To Millie

Apprenticed to M
*

A Memoir of Barbara Le Pard (2005 to 2010)
By
Geoff Le Pard

Copyright, etc.

Apprenticed To My Mother

Copyright 2018: Geoffrey Le Pard

For more information about the author and upcoming books, please visit geofflepard.com

Introduction

I had my fallouts with my father down the years, often silly, mostly temporary. The one that lasted longer than most ended when I married in May 1984. Even then it took another three years before we really settled all our, frankly, minor differences and began to develop the deep and lasting friendship that sustained us until his death. The forum for this rapprochement was a walking holiday with friends. When we set out, in June 1987, we imagined it to be a one-off. Over a decade of annual walking holidays later, we thought we would go on forever. These days our jaunts might be called "quality time" and I have many deeply embedded and much-loved memories to cherish from these holidays.

It wasn't the same with Mum. I never fell out with Mum but then again, I never had quite the same close relationship with her. As with so much in my family, conversations, experiences and the group mood were filtered through the prism of how Dad was feeling on any particular day. I was never really able to enjoy her exclusively, not while the old man was around.

So up to the point of his death, I thought of Mum as part of a double act, of them always together. It wasn't that she didn't have a personality, but rather that she deferred to him so often it was coloured by his presence.

And then he was gone, and we had to cope with an absence; more to the point, I had to cope with Mum. I was forty-nine and she... she wouldn't want me to tell you.

If you had asked me up to that point to describe Mum, it would have been clichéd: kind, funny, dutiful, family-orientated. But that would be, in its way, merely a caricature. It would have lacked real depth, without nuance. Too black and white.

What I didn't realise (I don't think either of us did) was that I was – and maybe we were - about to undertake yet another education, with the chosen subject being my mother.

This book is the story of that education. It is not a perfect chronological history of our five years, post Dad; indeed, there's little logic to it because there was no planning, nothing linear about how it unfolded. It is only in retrospect that I realise the indelible imprint Mum was, belatedly, leaving on me. And as I reflected I came to view other incidents, from an earlier time, in new ways. These have helped complete the picture of a woman of her time and of no time. She was unique – but aren't we all? However, within this distinctive picture of a charming, contrary, compassionate, curmudgeonly and caring parent, there is something universal, something from which we can all learn. That, I hope, is how you will find this story.

Necessarily, there is a fair bit about Dad too, and the rest of my family. With Dad, I have tried to give you a flavour of the man by including some of his poems; these come at the end of some of the chapters and I hope you enjoy them. A lot of them I only read for the first time after he died; he barred anyone but Mum from seeing them in his lifetime. Mum, however, was so very proud of them and him that this tribute to her would fail if I didn't also recognise his part, and, indeed, his skills, too.

My parents were married for fifty-three years; it should have been longer. I've often wondered at the gap between their first date, in the autumn of 1944, and their nuptials in March 1952. The War and Dad's service in Palestine kept them apart for three of those years but they spent the best part of four years, having corresponded assiduously during his absence in the Middle East, avoiding what I think all their friends and family would have assumed was inevitable.

It is not as if they had some libertarian objection to the institution of marriage, far from it. Nor was it money, I think. They weren't flush, but they both worked and there was always some help from Mum's mum, my gran. Reading some letters Dad wrote to Mum while away, in 1947/48, I would say he was very keen to "get spliced". I'm left to conclude that Mum decided the time wasn't ripe during those four years until, at last, it was. Though the eventual decision to wed would, I'm pretty certain, have been seen by all as prompted by Dad, I'm equally certain that he waited until Mum made it clear he could proceed.

This neatly encapsulates their marriage: on the one hand, Mum made sure no one ever pricked that bubble of masculine authority that Dad needed in order to feel whole, to be the man he aspired to be; at the same time, they both understood where the power resided so that, when it came to any crunch, the opinion that carried the day was Mum's, not that it ever needed articulating. A marriage of equals, in many ways, but the casting vote clearly resided with the mysterious feminine.

And then Dad died, in March 2005. I suppose we all expected there to be some changes, now she could, overtly at last, be in charge. The only problem was that Mum didn't want things to change. It is only looking back that I realise what she wanted most was someone to continue to play his role; maybe that way she could pretend, to some degree at least, that he was still there, still the figurehead, acting as her spokesperson in life.

That is why I stopped being her dutiful younger son, and instead I auditioned for the role as apprentice to the position of surrogate husband.

For those reading this memoir I must explain that I am reluctant to expose my lovely living family to any more scrutiny than is necessary in order to tell Mum's and, to an extent, Dad's story. So, you will meet, variously, the Textiliste (my wife), the Lawyer (my son), the Vet (my daughter), the Archaeologist (my brother) and others.

One

Driven To Distraction

We are told there are five stages of grief. After Dad died, the nearest Mum came to any of those five stages was a period of reflection, a withdrawal. She might nod occasionally to suggestions, answer questions about some issue around his estate, but otherwise she avoided indulging in anything like the classic steps. The Archaeologist and I always knew she would process her feelings in her own unique way and waited for her to emerge. I wondered what she would want to do first. What she would need from me, going forward? Maybe something physical, such as help clearing out some cupboards or something. I wasn't expecting her focus to be on, firstly the medical and, then, the mechanical.

I took a call one weekday morning, on my mobile, unusual as that was – to her, the mobile was associated with my work and she was loathe to interrupt me while I played at being important.

'Darling,' she began, 'I'm getting my knee done. I should have done it before but what with your father needing care...' She didn't need to complete the thought. After all, there was no way she would have incapacitated herself when he needed her most.

'Good. A little birdie told me it was giving you trouble.'

She made a dismissive noise, one with which I was to become very familiar. 'Your aunt should keep her own counsel.' Mum and her sister-in-law had what might be described as a full and frank relationship.

'She told me you were suffering a lot.'

'Phooey.' She was of a generation that didn't do pain; she fought it with her every fibre, so she could keep going.

'You're not in pain?'

Another tutt-snort combo of disdain. 'That's not the reason. Your father's clutch has decided to rebel.'

Like her knee, so it was with the family car. This, a Rover that Dad loved, suffered from neglect during his final two years which not only added to its creaks and groans but rendered its long-term future, at best, uncertain. It appeared that, despite the attentive ministrations of the local garage, the aforementioned clutch was so stiff, her compromised knee couldn't depress it enough to make the car go.

'I'll get my knee done and then we can sort out a new car.'

I was delighted. If Mum was planning for these two events she was beginning to focus on the future and dwelling less in the present. 'Excellent, Mum. Just let me know when you need my help.'

While the knee operation was successful in that it removed the pain, her recovery was slow as there was no one to nag her to do the necessary exercises. The garage did yet another temporary fix on the Rover but finally, some four months after Dad's funeral, I received another call. 'I'm getting rid of it.'

I knew what "it" was. It had become something of a constant in our conversations. 'Ok. Shall we go and have a look at options? I can come down at the weekend and…'

'I've found what I want. I just need some advice on trade-in values.'

I had to slow her down. The Archaeologist and I had already discussed this situation and we agreed we needed to try and persuade her to get an automatic. A committed driver, about to tip into her eightieth year with a recent knee replacement, didn't need the constant stress that a clutch pedal imposed, even if new and smooth. I floated the idea.

'Why would I want an automatic? Your father thought them unmanly.'

He probably did, but he never told me. 'It would be easier.'

'In the war we drove ten tonne trucks with none of your power steering.'

'That was over sixty years ago, Mum.'

'Doreen put me off automatics.' Mum was excellent at moving the argument on if she felt her base becoming less than solid.

'Doreen?'

'She's this year's President.' In Mum's world the only President that mattered was whoever held that post for the Hordle Women's Institute, a formidable organisation of local women who made jam and swapped suggestions on the subtle art of husband manipulation. 'She listened to her son and look what happened to her. Such a sensible woman should have known better.' This was quite a criticism, since the received wisdom locally was that a WI President was invested, on elevation, with a sagacity that would have made Aristotle pea-green with envy.

I began to back down. When she started a conversation about people I didn't know it usually meant I was about to be outflanked, but Mum was nothing if not a terrier with its blood up when she thought she

7

was winning. 'She bought an automatic and ended up in the hairdresser's.'

'I'm sorry?'

'So was Doreen. Imagine if it had been a school.'

'Can we back up? What do you mean "she ended up in the hairdresser's"?'

Was that tone one of exasperation that I didn't understand or a smug realisation she had me where she wanted me? 'Just that. She took this fancy-dan automatic you love so much to get her weekly wash and set – we were having a jam-making day, so she had to look right – and was leaving when the car took over as she tried to reverse. It shot backwards, like a cork from one of your father's infernal Calvados imports and ended up back in the hairdresser's. Jean–Claude said he nearly self-permed he was so shocked. If it wasn't for the reception desk stopping the dratted car, we might never again get to enjoy Mrs Hudson's Caramel Three Tiered. Not that she'll be up to baking much until she recovers her composure. Apparently, she was showered in so much glass she looked like a nonagenarian glitter-ball.'

'Creep.'

She tutted. 'I know he's a little camp, and he may well be homo-wotsit, but really, darling, you shouldn't call the hairdresser a creep. That's not very enlightened.'

'Not Jean-Claude. The car. Automatics creep. Makes reversing tricky if you don't practice.'

More tutting, 'The point is I'm too old to learn such a delicate skill. I'll stick with proper gears, thank you. Anyway, I've paid for it.'

Pause.

'It is French. A Peugeot.'

This last was said with some hesitation. And a tincture of guilt. "Buying foreign" was not something of which Mum approved. Nor did Dad.

'A Peugeot? They're a good make. I'm sure it will be fine.'

'Your father would have had something to say.'

Indeed, he would. We both fell silent, imagining his reaction to hearing Mum had bought a French car. Dad loved France and all things French. When he was there. But on this side of the Channel? Not so much. I waited for her to speak, knowing she was probably talking to him about it, no doubt reassuring his memory that it was a good deal. Value for money would usually trump national pride.

'So, trade-in values on the Rover? Do you think I should hold out for more than two hundred and fifty pounds?'

We debated pros and cons though she had already decided to accept it. She was merely making me feel as if I had been useful. That was to become something of a theme.

Then, as we were about to end the call, she added, 'Oh and I've ordered two deaf-aids.'

Now that was a result. Her hearing wasn't too bad, at least not as bad as Dad's, but it was beginning to fade and we, the family, had dropped some hints, though she probably hadn't heard them. I told her Dad would have been pleased; bringing his approval into a conversation always meant we ended on a happy note.

Little did I realise then how that car and those deaf aids would combine to test my sanity. That is for later. For now, though, I was pleased she was taking steps into the future, not merely marking time in the present. It had taken us a while to reach this point as we shall see.

Two

The End And The Beginning

I'm not sure when the morbid thought first hit me. Probably about the time I began to feel I was becoming my parents' reluctant sounding board. I didn't ask for or relish any role in their decision-making processes. Nonetheless, I was allocated that position of responsibility-without-power one day – I must have missed the meeting – and forever after they 'sought' my opinion, something they had eschewed for the first four decades of my life. When I say they "sought" it I don't mean they listened especially well, for they rarely did what I suggested if it didn't happen to accord with their thinking. I did wonder why they bothered asking me; I reckoned they liked to have someone with whom to share the blame if things went wrong, but maybe they did genuinely want a second opinion. Sometimes.

In fact, there was the beginnings of a reliance and I could only see it going one way. To the extent I thought about it at all, I assumed it would be practical support; the sort that comprised help-with-shopping, pretend-I-understood-DIY kind of thing. If anyone, back then, had suggested the support might be more intellectual or, heaven forbid, emotional, I'd have thought them rather ridiculous. They clearly didn't know my parents.

But things were moving on. They wondered if they should go on holiday and only decided to after I pressed them to grasp the opportunity. They then thanked me for helping make up their minds. Yes, my status was changing and, as the occasions for my advice being sought and taken increased so did the need for a bit of recalibration.

Which, inexorably, led to my thinking this morbid thought:

Given the statistical likelihood that they will not die together which parent do I want to survive?

I know. Dreadful, isn't it? But I was being realistic, and brutally so. On the one hand, I had always done more with Dad, and had more in common with him, than with Mum. Superficially, he would be easy company, easy to please and probably, despite the fluster and bluster, reasonably malleable. On the other hand, Mum was self-reliant. She wouldn't need cosseting; I wouldn't panic about her feeding herself or changing a fuse or buying too many envelopes and not enough toilet rolls. One would be fun and high maintenance; the other easy to manage if something of an enigma. Can a parent I've known all my life be an enigma? For sure. It didn't take much consideration to appreciate that, even though they were patently equals in their marriage, family news, opinions and most of the conversations were filtered through Dad's story-telling machine. How well, I asked myself, did I know Mum? Would she really be so easy to manage?

I was a very busy lawyer trying to pretend I was also an involved parent. The idea of having to parent my father more than I was already doing seemed too much of an extra burden so logic said, if one has to go, and, truly, I didn't want either to, it had to be Dad.

That it was the way it happened, well, it didn't make it any better.

I run thought experiments all the time; what-if scenarios, if you like. That's great if you're a writer, but it feels a bit creepy and sick when applied to family and survival. Having thought the thought, I imagined what the world, post-Dad, would be like. Neat. Compact. Structured. Understandable. Logical. Not much stress.

Of course, I never communicated to Mum how I viewed such a scenario, and, of course, it was never going to be as I imagined it. Neither did she let on that, in these specific circumstances, what she needed - what she expected - was not a caring son giving helpful advice, but a better, new and improved version of her husband – Desmond 2.0. A version that did away with the huffing and puffing and mild ranting, and fell in with whatever her thinking was after having been given the semblance of a voice. Diligent, compliant, available when needed but absent when not.

Unknowingly I had applied to be her apprentice and had got the gig.

Three

The Mum List

Being an apprentice wasn't a role with which I was unfamiliar. Back in my teens, my mother decided the Archaeologist and I needed a set of skills that would stand us in good stead when we were released into the world.

Take cooking. Mum loved to cook. That doesn't really do justice to the importance of food in her life. She loved to be the creator of comfort and food featured highly in that equation. When I was a child she tended to a fairly traditional menu of British staples: roasts and home-grown vegetables; puddings to add ballast; fried and grilled flesh of all kinds; and tea, lots of tea.

The selection depended, as so much did, on my father's current philosophy - perhaps prejudice would have been nearer the mark - and as his focus widened so did his tastes. A tin of curry powder appeared circa 1971, along with the assumption that it didn't matter what you curried, the spices remained the same. Then pasta joined in - spaghetti at first then penne, but the sauces stayed largely of the Bolognese disposition until the 1990s. There followed exotic and not universally successful experiments involving kidney beans (fairly explosive), chow mein (too viscous) and artichoke (seriously explosive).

Mum knew we needed to have at least a modicum of culinary skills to survive and set about ensuring both we boys understood the basics and, she hoped, joined her in her love of this kind of creativity. She started with boiling an egg and cutting soldiers and then moved us steadily, stealthily forward. With Mum, as with most things, she took her time to expand our range.

Indeed, you could see this incremental approach - my parents' culinary journey, if you like - in their relationship with alcohol. When I appeared in the 1950s, beer would have been my father's staple. And that's the flat warm ale beloved of old men in pubs and trendy micro-brewers residing, mole-like, under railway arches, and not the fizzy amber dishwater that passed for lager back then. If he felt flush he might have had a whisky - a blend like Bells, not then anything as subtle as a single malt - and if he felt sophisticated it would be a G&T. Mum drank the G&Ts too but also port and, at Christmas, a yellow by-product of medical experiments called Warninks Advocaat. The only saving grace about this sweet sharp gunk was the glacé cherry that floated on the top and which, if I behaved, Mum would let me steal.

Come the 1970s wine had become increasingly evident. To begin it was distinguished solely by colour. Whites, usually capable of immobilising mammoths, and reds that must have been sponsored by Dyno Rod as they certainly cleared the sluices. Gradually wine categorisation narrowed: French = sophisticated; German = sweet and cheap; Australian = not taken seriously. Then finally we had a Côtes du Rhone and the die had been cast. By the time Dad died I'd say spirits had retreated, though scotch had been replaced by a taste for Calvados, and while beer still featured in the right company, it was wine that was making a bid for the top spot.

Inevitably Mum and Dad tried to make their own, with no noticeable success. Do not believe anyone if they say oak leaves can be made into wine. They can be made into floor cleaner or one of those mysterious unguents that my grandmother used for her rheumatics and which made her whimper at the same time as walking quickly with her legs oddly apart. But fit for human consumption? I think not.

Mum knew we'd be inclined to learn to cook if we believed meal creation was fun. As boys we made fudge and fondants, biscuits and cakes. Then buns and breads - making Chelsea buns was a popular choice.

And so it was that we boys were gradually introduced to the Mum List and her lessons in "How to be a man". The philosophy behind the List was to imbue us with

a set of skills that all young men should have but which your father hasn't

and which, come what may the Archaeologist and I had to acquire before we left home. So far as she was concerned she was not going to allow us loose in the world and in particular, prey on some unsuspecting but probably gullible female as ill-equipped to survive as Dad had been when she fell for him. As examples of the more critical skills on the List, we had to learn how to:

- Iron a shirt and fold same
- Ditto a pair of suit trousers using a damp cloth to create a sharp crease
- Cook three meals involving meat, fish and a pie and three puddings
- Wash clothes (no washing machine allowed) including handkerchiefs

- Rewire a plug
- Make a bed
- Pack a suitcase
- Put up a shelf
- Clean a bathroom (and why)
- Check the vital signs of the internal combustion engine viz oil and water levels, spark plugs and tyre pressures

There were other skills I failed to acquire: changing a tap washer, for instance, but if we exhibited a degree of competence in the principle items, we were forgiven our inabilities elsewhere.

In Dad's final year, and, indeed after his death, Mum's love of cooking faded somewhat, but in a way it provided a neat example of how things needed to change, if my apprenticeship was going to progress. Previously I would arrive at the family home and settle down with Dad to put the world to rights while Mum provided endless sustenance. Now, in his absence, it was with Mum that these initial conversations took place. By now she was in her late seventies, yet she'd usher me into her kitchen, sit me down and make tea while asking questions of her grandchildren's latest doings. She'd then start cooking a meal. Unconsciously, since this is what had happened forever in my life - from coming home from school to returning from university and later visiting with my own family - I let her potter around her domain, talking, listening and cooking, readying to be fed and watered.

It was the Textiliste who articulated what should have been obvious. 'Aren't you going to help your mum?'

The Textiliste wasn't always able to join me on my visits south so didn't always see what happened on my arrival. But sometime soon after Dad's death, she watched with, I suspect, a degree of horror as I slumped back in the seat and chatted with Mum, waiting to be waited on.

Chastised, I stood to join in; Mum tried to stop me. Only briefly and without much resistance. She wasn't cross with her daughter-in-law; not at all. I think, for her, by my sitting and allowing myself to be waited upon, I served the purpose of reminding her of Dad, of how he couldn't really function without her. And how the centre of their world was the kitchen even if her truly happy place was her garden.

She let me help as I would henceforth - she understood male guilt better than most - but she would have preferred I stayed put and let her pretend, for just a little while longer, that something of her beloved

Des still remained nearby. Becoming an apprentice was going to challenge us both.

Four

Coping

Dad's final illness lasted about a year and in that time Mum did nothing but care for him. The final six weeks of his life were pretty grim. He knew – everyone knew – it was going to end soon: he was bed-ridden, and he spent most of the time in Poole hospital rather than a local hospice (to which we tried and failed to get him admitted). That meant a daily commute of twenty miles each way for Mum with which my family helped, but if no one was available, then she drove herself. None of us knew how much her knee hurt – she needed to have the joint replacing desperately – but she wasn't telling anyone because her focus was elsewhere.

As had been her default position in life to put others first, so those last months distilled her personality to its most fundamental: keep calm and be the rock around which everyone else could dance and cry and weep and wail. She never cried or raised her voice; she remained placid and logical throughout. Watching her watching him as he faded was to see stoicism in its most poignant, most beautiful form.

After sixty-two years of togetherness and love and knowing you'll be the one remaining, the one making do, and at no point did self-pity enter her soul. She needed a lot of hugs, mind you. And tea. You can hide in tea.

I suppose I assumed, when he finally died in the early hours of 12th March 2005, that the effort would leave her drained and in need of a rest. But her attention was immediately on her family, especially the Archaeologist and me, on making sure we coped. She wanted his memory to be of the fun-giving man and, in her quiet but rigorous way, she was going to make sure no one was going to change that. And she didn't want us to worry about her. She refused to be a burden, victim or anything other than independent. I'm not sure I could manage such poise.

Me? I hid in paperwork. My head admired her resilience while my heart wanted to explode. But how could I be the burden, go to pieces if she didn't? So, I opened his bureau and delved into their paper lives. And I found that – while I knew Mum hoarded everything and fought a battle with Dad, who ostensibly wanted a regular clear out of what he considered clutter, when it came to their financial affairs - he was as bad as her. There were bank statements going back thirty years, details of pension plans and P60s covering decades. Tax codes and premium bonds, shares from privatisations and ISAs and Tessas and deeds and receipts. Oh, those bloody receipts. I could have made a papier mâché life-sized sculpture of the old sod from those scraps.

We needed to sort out a funeral. However, before that and while I was deep into checking on death certificates and so on, Mum appeared at my side, clutching an old shoe box. It contained all his poetry, all the poems he swore I would never see – "Just mush, boy, soppy stuff". She wanted me to find something suitable for the funeral, but more than that she wanted me to understand him a little better.

Every year, for over twenty-five years, he wrote her a poem on her birthday. We all sort of knew he did something, but these love poems were beautiful. They were funny at times, rude too, but always they echoed his love for her and hers for him.

This was a test of sorts, part of the selection process to determine my suitability to become her apprentice. What did I intend to do with them? I told her I wanted to have them properly typed up and turned into a small book to be made available to the friends and family who attended the funeral. She was thrilled. I was moved onto the shortlist.

That was the easy bit - a PA at work kindly typed them all up and I had them bound. The difficult part was choosing which three would form part of his funeral service. I needed to reflect the man but not embarrass him, as judged by Mum. Even in death she wanted him to be comfortable with whatever it was that we revealed. His human side, yes, but not so much that in life would have made him squirm, if read aloud. On this she and I disagreed.

We took time rehearsing the arguments, the good reasons to do it her way and mine.

And we did it her way. Of course. Mostly.

The first was easy and the one on which we didn't disagree. His A Paratrooper's Prayer, written to his mother in 1945 when he was about to take his first ever jump – he was just about eighteen – was fabulous, and we both knew would ensure there wouldn't be a dry eye in the house.

A Paratrooper's Prayer

When I'm flying at seven hundred
And the red-light flickers on

17

I know I'll tremble and start to sweat
But, God, let me be strong.

*

When I look down through the hole, God
It's like standing by a grave
And my knees go weak and I can't speak
Then, God, please make me brave.

*

And if it be Thy Will, God
Part of Thine Own Great Plan
That my life should stop, then on that last long drop
Oh God, let me die a man!

*

While I'm waiting to emplane, God
And I'm checking my jumping kit
Though I laugh and jeer I'm full of fear
But, God don't let me quit.

*

When the kite begins to move, God
And take off time is near
Then my heart grows cold - God, make me bold
And drive away my fear.

But the other two? Tricky. She wanted humour and cliché; I wanted the humour but also to reflect his love of her. Goodness that was hard, finding one; in the end a poem about her garden, one of his Barbara has gone into the garden again poems was selected, probably against her initial better judgment. The look, as she acceded to my pleadings told of the risk I was taking; if I had judged the mood of the audience wrongly, if anyone hinted at any sort of sneering, if anyone said, "well, that surprised me", or "I never expected Des to be such an old romantic", then my new role might be still-born.

18

Five

Into The Woods

I had many things in common with my father: a love of sport; a tendency to explode with frustration and then humble myself with guilt immediately after; and, and this annoyed (and still annoys) the treasured women in our lives, a stupid fixation with arguing with the radio, which both of us understood was irrational and futile, but neither of us could (or in my case, can) stop it.

There was another character trait, too: DIY incompetence and, especially, when it comes to making something from wood. I'm not entirely clear what prompted it – perhaps recompense for yet another explosive outburst – but in about 1964 Dad agreed to make Mum a glass fronted cabinet for our sitting room. Being that "white heat of technology" time, one of my parents, Dad probably, determined it would be made from the latest laminate and be in the style of the still fashionable G-plan furniture.

I remember the trip to the timber yard to buy the wood because of the agonising over what exact type and colour of wood to pick. I can well imagine how the Archaeologist would have needed pacifying since his level of patience never stretched far in those days, unless it involved a trip to a museum or library. But if there was a delay in the buying of the wood, it was as nothing to how long it took for the same to be converted into the cabinet. Every weekend for an age, some argument would ensue, often starting or ending with the cabinet, or rather its lack, being utilised by one or other to try and win some point.

It did get built, but the deep emotional and psychological scarring proved too much for Dad. Thus it was that when Mum suggested building a cupboard under the stairs to house things like his tools and the vacuum cleaner, Dad turned pale and had to sit down.

Male feebleness, however, was never going to be allowed as an excuse. Once it was clear Dad was not going to buy the timber needed, Mum measured up and bought everything herself. The wood stood propped in the space where the cupboard was to go, collecting dust and foul looks in equal measure. I really think Mum expected Dad's deep well of guilt, when mixed with male ego, to be sufficient to motivate him to take on the task. But she hadn't reckoned with such unexpected stubbornness. He held out; she cajoled; he demurred; she pleaded. Impasse. Stasis.

Then something broke; some unspoken rule in the game of marital management. Dad went off to play rugby, crawling back in the wee hours full of hop and bonhomie. He was practiced in the art of slipping into bed quietly, only this particular night he hadn't factored in Mum reaching the end of what had, up to that point, been an infinitely elastic tether.

'Ow! What the bloody hell...?'

Everyone was awake. Two worried boys peered into their parents' bedroom at two angry parents. I don't think either of us understood who was the angrier; all we could see was that Dad's side of the bed had been filled with two by four planking and about one hundred steel screws. Not so much apple-pied as apple-treed.

Nothing was said about this mysterious incident the next day, or subsequently. The wood was back in the space under the stairs by the morning. But there was a shift in the dynamic. Coming home from school on the following Monday, Mum was not to be found in the garden, nor in the kitchen. Exploring deeper into the house we found her, drill in hand, sticking batons on the wall. From then on, if anything needed to be done around the house or garden, involving wood, Mum did it.

All this is a roundabout way to consider the next stage in my apprenticeship. We were told we could organise for the body to be collected, but we had to decide how we were going to deal with it. My grandmothers, the last two deaths in the family, had both been cremated in Bournemouth. There was something blandly functional about these ceremonies. They lacked, well, any form of ceremony. More a utilitarian disposal. Everyone was kind, considered and considerate, but the sense of motions being gone through was as ever present as a gas leak. No, Dad deserved better.

My aunt turned out to be the saviour. She and my uncle had organised plots at a woodland burial site, when your body would become compost to feed a tree of your choice, to be planted, in lieu of a headstone, a'top your grave. That, in the blink of an eye, was the solution.

And there, too, was the irony. Dad would forever after be associated with wood, a substance as far from his comfort zone as singing an aria and skinny-dipping in the round pond on Clapham Common. At least any idea Mum may have had that she should compost the old boy in the back garden – and none of us would have put it past her – was shelved for this more formalised recycling.

Getting someone buried is, frankly, a faff. We chose an oak tree – a very English oak tree – to be planted on top of his grave which would be fed by years of investment in Wadsworth's 6X and Ringwood Ales. At the same time, Mum bought the neighbouring plot so she could be buried next to him. I tried to think that was efficient and, perhaps, rather sweet, but it also seemed too sensible, just then. I wanted to stop thinking about my parents' mortality for a while. Not that you are allowed such a luxury when you have a burial to organise.

Dad's poems, until that is we were shown his complete collection, tended to the epic-historical or the humorous. Let us start with one he wrote for a friend's birthday, which deals with aging, a theme he dwelt on quite a bit.

Life In An Old Dog

When a man grows old and the fire goes cold
Down in the boiler room,
And he can't remember how to fan the embers,
He's inclined to lapse into gloom.
*

But such melancholy is unnecessary folly,
And may easily be cured,
By bearing in mind the solace he can find
In the warm, and the ripe, and the matured.
*

For a roll in the hay, in the month of May,
Though exciting, was not always a success,
But a delicate affaire when the trees are bare
Can be rewarding – and a lot less stress!

Six

Band Leader

After the method and location of the internment were determined, the next piece of admin was to identify someone to run the ceremony – a master of ceremonies, I suppose. The Archaeologist and I would have been quite happy to do it all ourselves, but the rules of the burial ground dictated an independent third party. Their excuse was to ensure the dignity of the occasion which made me wonder at some of the ceremonies they had had before such a rule was introduced. Unfortunately, I couldn't shake the idea that it was for a far more expedient reason – we had a timed slot and they wanted us in and out, or maybe in and under, in the agreed window. No long-winded, maudlin reminiscences were going to be tolerated, I suspected.

My parents lived on the outskirts of a small village, Hordle, on the edge of the New Forest in southern England. While my mother was a card-carrying atheist and had a long-running grumble with all the many incumbents as local vicar down the years – the pillars of village power were the church and the Women's Institute where Mum undertook the role of horticultural Machiavelli – she knew Dad had a sort of embarrassed Anglicanism as a faith. Dad liked to pretend he was a rebel, but, like Brighton rock, he had "conformity" written through his veins. Which meant we needed some member of the cloth to mastermind the ceremony.

We found a suitable candidate – someone who had not come across Mum - who came to talk to us about Dad. The sweet woman soon realised her role was merely as prompt to the Archaeologist and me. It was our show, something Mum was very pleased to encourage. 'If it keeps the mumbo-jumbo to a minimum,' she muttered rather unhelpfully during our get to know you session.

There's a lot to be done at these times. Organising the release of the body, obtaining the death certificate, agreeing on the funeral arrangements, letting people know of the death and the subsequent date for the final farewell – I found I had to allow for a significant investment of time when I made contact with his old friends, colleagues and family as they were all very kind, wanting to share some happy memory. But I just wanted to get on. Time enough to reminisce later.

I think it was during the trip to Bournemouth to register the death and obtain the death certificate that I noticed the first change in Mum. While outwardly she remained polite – too polite for a woman whose sotto voce mutterings had embarrassed me for decades – I realised she hadn't engaged in the detail of the conversation with the registrar.

It would be easy to assume this was a one-off. Dealing explicitly with his death would inevitably bring on a suppressed sadness in any mortal. But Mum was never "any mortal". She didn't give in to emotion. Ever.

Yet she had definitely begun to withdraw, to do the minimum to let people think she was coping while in practice she shut down all extraneous functions.

And I was glad. Glad she was giving herself some of her time rather than worrying about others. Glad I could take over. Glad she could stop being quite so brave. Glad I could be the strong one for a bit. It made it easier to cope, knowing I had to do it for her.

As we approached the funeral my mood definitely changed. Ok, we were about to bury someone I loved dearly, but in celebrating a life, we were also going to do what Dad loved above all else: we were going to have one mother of a party. If Dad was in his element – and I saw no reason why he wouldn't be there, at his own wake – it was in a crowd with a glass of something distilled in one hand.

On Mum's last birthday before Dad died, when they both knew pretty well this would be the last one they would celebrate together, he wrote her this poem. I'd have read it out at his funeral despite Mum's inevitable protestations, save for the fact I never found it until after she died. I might be a pillar of the legal establishment, but I was fifty percent from her gene pool and therefore not to be trusted completely. It was, for her, too raw I think. But she knew I'd find it and share it and that was ok; just as long as she could meet his gaze in their own little green and verdant Valhalla and know she'd not let him down after he'd gone. I could, but she wouldn't. So here it is now: sorry, Mum. And, Dad.

October 21st, 2004

Life is fleeting but love's eternal
And we are proving it, you and I
For these are magical moments my love
And I try so hard not to cry.
*

Those secret smiles which only I share
Your laughter which means so much
Together bound with a golden thread
Your loving, gentle touch.
*

I just couldn't let your birthday pass
Or let emotion overcome
So, thanks my love for a wonderful life
Now, tomorrow, here we come!!

Seven

A Final Word

The day was overcast. Rain threatened. A warm, sort of decaying, damp day. Fungoid. Dad would approve. 'Let's go and see if we can find some mushrooms.' To which he would inevitably add, 'And pupae.' A couple of hours of chit and chat as we strolled amongst his memories on his beloved New Forest and then a pint of something hoppy. That would be a perfect day for him.

That would be ideal for his funeral too. Friends, chat, laughs, beer. Or as near as we could recreate it.

But as well as the above, you are expected to have songs, or at least music.

That was a challenge, agreeing three pieces. He never talked about his funeral. Understandable, of course. Never gave us a hint. And he wasn't especially musical, either. This meant Mum, the Archaeologist and I had to agree on what was suitable. We could have selected one piece each, but Mum would have had the final say. Of course. It's funny; I remember the effort of choosing, of the discussion we had but not the outcome. Two pieces were easily selected: What a Wonderful World by Louis Armstrong and Glen Miller's In The Mood.

But what was to be the third piece? He said he enjoyed Abba – the short skirts I think – but somehow Dancing Queen didn't convey the man we knew. My Way? Too cheesy. Jerusalem? Too WI. Always Look on the Bright Side? Too modern. Indeed, so difficult was it, I can't now recall what we went for. Maybe we just stopped at two.

It's so easy to forget the details of the day, with so much emotion wrapped up in it. The day was episodic anyway, with the emphasis on the "sod" as in "it was a sod of a day". Did I speak first or the Archaeologist? Did it rain? Did everyone come? Did we eat sandwiches or rolls? It's like a Swiss cheese, my memory of that day, even though I was a main player.

I remember I bottled one aspect. Dressing him. That would have meant seeing him dead, so I left it to Mum. Mum wanted to, so she chose what might be thought of as his formal dress: cream slacks, blue blazer, with silver buttons, white shirt and the Parachute Regiment tie – he was proud to call himself a "Para". I'd have done it differently - walking gear, with the tie used as a belt - had it been my decision. Mum would have hated the disrespect that using his tie that way suggested, but I was pretty sure he'd have understood the joke. It's probably as well we didn't debate this, because he could be quite contrary and we both knew he'd be hovering over us on the day, making his presence felt. After all, on such a difficult day, you want it friction-free, really, don't you?

My parents' marriage was as solid as a rock, for which I will forever be grateful and they were delighted when I married the Textiliste for any number of good reasons. At our wedding, despite the fact it was not customary for the father of the groom to say anything, Dad was encouraged, by Mum, to share this poem. Inevitably it veers towards the jokey and slightly cheesy, but it came with such oodles of love there weren't many dry eyes left. And it is perhaps apposite to see it here, reflecting as it did Dad's belief in my innate and irredeemable scruffiness, to be counterpointed by his own dapper elegance which I'm sure Mum maintained that final time.

Geoffrey and Linda – Wedding 1984

In the year of Our Lord 1956 there were Tories in No. 10
Arthur Scargill, no doubt, was already about,
And Wedgewood was still hyphen Benn.
*

Not every young man had a car and for transport they got their bikes out
But fellas in shorts still harboured rude thoughts
About girls on settees with the lights out.
*

Mini-skirts were about to be thought of – uncovering some of the mystery,
And then tights came in – men thought it a sin
When stocking tops just became history.
*

On Saturday nights lads wore ties – not bracelets or earrings or lockets,
And these boozers in suits could get pickled as coots
On just 'the pound in their pockets'.
*

In those days, we still used real money and five bob meant two seats at the flicks
But young men on the Town were surprised when they found
What they got for nineteen and six.
*

All this is by way of preamble, a little scene setting seemed needful,
For most we remember a day in November
When the stork came with Geoff – what a beakful!

28

*

He was just a normal small boy, with a natural aversion to water,
And when dressed in his best he still looked a mess
And we knew we hadn't a daughter.
*

Sport was the love of his life, especially cricket and rugger,
And like all small boys he was grubby and noisy
He could be an awkward young b****r!
*

As he grew up he got worse – terrified me and his mother
And we're amazed to this day how they got away
With the things they did, him and his brother!
*

And so in the fullness of time, to Bristol he went, to read Law
For three years he stayed there, worked there and played there
And of one thing we're very sure.
*

That although he had great times at Bristol – certainly we heard no
moans,
His greatest success as I'm sure you can guess
Was to woo, and to win, Linda Jones.
*

So Lin and Geoff life is just starting, and the years will reward you –
and test you
But on your wedding day I would just simply say,
Dear Geoff and dear Linda – God bless you.

Eight

Happy Hour

While I may have difficulty recalling certain aspects of Dad's funeral, the one thing that sticks is that there was a lot of talking. Being talked at and talking myself, though what I said, well a lot of that has gone. In advance, my aim had been to make it happy, a clichéd celebration. I know that some of what I said generated a few laughs and the occasional dab of an eye. I recall a sense of satisfaction as well as being a bit cheap, maybe playing him for laughs. It was my version of a send-off, not his and not Mum's. Later she said she liked it and thanked me profusely, but at the time I noticed both smiles and frowns. When she smiled, I think she shut her eyes, but sometimes she seemed to recognise the man I tried to capture in a few words. It's a bit blurry so I might be wrong and, in truth, she may well not have been focusing on my words at all. That's understandable, of course.

Inevitably I've thought about the funeral since. I know she was very grateful that I read his poems without losing it, giving them a proper chance to shine. What I think I may not have pitched quite right were the anecdotes. And that's probably because the man I wanted to describe was the one whose ability to prick his own pomposity saved him from being insufferable. If Dad had one trait above all others that brought you back to him after he had said something to piss you off – he could be as irritating as viral nits – it was his ability to laugh at himself. His biggest joke was always himself and some of the best, most well-loved of the stories about him had him as the centre of the funny.

On that fated day, when I told a story, with me as the joke and Dad as the hero, Mum closed her eyes, and maybe nodded. But for her, telling something about Dad at his funeral, at the going down of his own little bit of sun, then that has to respect the man she loved; perhaps some were not what she really wanted because they didn't do that completely. At least not in her eyes. I gave myself a B+ and probably I was being generous. Dad would have laughed, though.

Mum was back being Mum that day and making sure everyone was comfortable, so I'd never know. If someone cried, she was there to comfort them. If someone lost their words, Mum filled in. She took the condolences offered with a gentleness and sincerity that helped people feel as if they'd said something useful and special, not, as is often the

30

case, something trite and repetitive. She surrounded my father's bereft family and friends in a kapok of love and a lake of tea.

My most vivid memory is by the grave, looking at a dark hole and wondering if he'd have planted potatoes or runners in it before concluding he'd have lined it with old newspaper and planted sweet peas.

His coffin was a wicker box, that wobbled disconcertingly, much like a few lips. I held Mum's arm and she squeezed mine. 'Bye, darling,' she whispered at that box before she moved to her grandchildren and held them in turn. I don't like graves, I decided. Too gloomy; no obvious laughs.

I worried about the immediate "after". How would she deal with the ungraspable future, stretching who knew where? The focus of the funeral had gone, so what next?

An empty house that would remain empty. Her solution was to buy two more small radios and leave them on in different rooms, tuned inevitably to Radio Four. The incessant chatter, the tone, heard at a distance, like something between a rant and a fit of giggles, replicated life with the old boy around.

She had plenty of support from family who lived locally, and friends, delightful, if somewhat intimidating, members of the Women's Institute. But even so, once the funeral was done, she began to withdraw, to avoid engaging in anything that smacked of the "future". She'd deal with the now only. It may have been imperceptible to many, but to those closest to her, it was as if her batteries needed recharging. Or maybe replacing.

I took more time off. I pottered around, beginning the process of sorting out his estate, and watched her move fully into this new stage that I first spotted at the Registrar's.

For instance, there would be no tears. I knew she wouldn't cry. Never ever would you see Mum cry. 'I cried when Daddy died' - that was 1940 - 'and I'm all cried out,' she once told me. Nor would there be self-pity. But a period of introspection? Yes, I thought that likely. I just had to keep things functioning and wait on a sign.

There would be an end and a new beginning. Not exactly a coming to terms and certainly not a release. Just be patient, I thought, hold back on those mounting questions, give her a minute or ten.

It took maybe three months. And when she was ready, she revealed it in her own particular way. The announcement contained the seeds of what was to come. It was during the phone call about her knee and the car. And it contained the classic "mumism". 'Your father wouldn't listen.'

It was the "Your father". Not "my husband" or "Des". Her comment involved a criticism of her now deceased husband and – this was something I was to learn about my role as her apprentice – I was to be linked in some way to whatever the failure, or failing, or perceived weakness was that she wanted to correct or resolve. Yep, my mother was back, she was firing, and my life with her was about to become very different.

Another birthday poem, from 1985

To Barbara – On her birthday, 21 October 1985 (Her sixtieth)

Thanks, My Love, for all these years,
So often smiles, so seldom tears,
Thanks, too, for many, many joys.
(Thanks especially for the boys!)
The house, the garden – everywhere
I look and know that you've been there.
Alone, I'm just an also-ran,
But when you're here then I'm a Man.
You're my lover, friend, companion, wife,
Dear Barbs – you are my very life.

Nine

Quarts And Pint Pots

After the knee and the car, the stage was set for the big one: the downsize.

The family home had been, since 1969, a New Forest "cottage". This brings to mind a twee, roses round the door, low-beamed, ancient homestead with pigs, an Aga and a well for water.

In fact, it was a four-bedroom jerry-built Edwardian villa prone to damp and with disconcertingly wobbly chimneys. My parents bought it because of its relative isolation and the potential of the third of an acre to become the garden my mother desired.

For nearly forty years they patched the house, trying various expedients to keep out the damp and keep in the heat while they gardened – actually, it was more like alchemy – and created their triangle of paradise.

Shit, it was hard work. I'm sure my parents paid lip-service to the Lords Mansfield, Shaftesbury and Fox and their campaigns to eradicate slavery but, while sound in theory, they didn't believe in freeing their own children from horticultural indentures.

Of my father's many aphorisms, his favourite – and the Archaeologist will attest to this – was "You don't keep a dog and bark yourself" alongside "Don't clap, throw money" and "Always leave them laughing".

We dug that barren patch of desert to a depth equivalent to the mid-Atlantic and wheel-barrowed and bucketed the resulting slimy clay across the road, there to dump it into the tangled mess of vegetation. Of course, this wasn't our land, but equally no one ever showed any interest in it so that was all right then. Wasn't it?

Some twenty years later the farm and fields opposite were sold, including the strip of neglected verge onto which our small mountain had been dumped. The new owner asked Dad if he'd ever seen anyone fly-tipping clay there. Somehow Dad kept a straight face as he sympathised with our new neighbour, agreeing that standards had dropped a long way with the advent of unleaded petrol, universal suffrage and novelty condoms. Had I been there and not had this reported to me later, I would have shopped my parents. Justice was never done.

Indeed, I harbour a less than secret grudge against Princess Anne and her first wedding in 1973 to the unchinned Captain Phillips. We had a day off school which happened to coincide with a ton of very fresh cow manure being delivered. The farm hand merely emptied his trailer on the road outside our house, advised Mum to tell disconcerted motorists to treat it as a roundabout and left for the pub. Mum feared some reputational damage from the existence of this festering, glutinous heap and set the Archaeologist and me to barrowing it down the garden. So rather than a day free to spend with my mates, I moved muck.

The void we created by our clay excavations was also filled with a constant supply of pony and horse crap collected from wherever she spotted it, leaf mould from under the many deciduous trees on the Forest, some peat from the many marshy areas dotted thereabouts and all sorts of fibrous growing materials that Mum procured by fair means and foul. Talking of fowl, if I have one piece of advice for nascent gardeners it is this: if offered goose faeces as some sort of superior guano, AVOID at all costs, unless you possess a state-of-the-art gas-mask; though taking positives from my one experience of digging this specific form of shit, you will never again suffer from blocked sinuses.

The combination of all this was a growing compost to die for and, by 1975, my parents' new empire was taking shape. In terms of timing, I left for university that year – the Archaeologist went the year before - so the exploitation was completed just in time. Coincidence, perhaps?

From there on it was one round of beauteous advancement after another. Mum and Dad were rightly praised for this transformation, but I think we should acknowledge some personal cost. I cannot prove this, but both the Archaeologist and I were each estimated, aged eight, to be likely to grow to at least six feet two inches tall; we both stopped growing during the Manure Years and while we each of us had a growth spurt of sorts at uni, we neither of us made it past five feet eleven.

Dad's poems beginning "Barbara has gone into the garden again" told a universal truth. Life was not always easy or settled back in the 1970s. My mother had rheumatoid arthritis diagnosed in the mid-1960s and her knees often caused her a lot of grief, not that she showed it much.

But when things weighed down too heavily she would slip outside together with her trug full of tools, her transistor radio, and potter about as best she could. If depression was ever likely it was kept at bay by rigorous pruning and a constant attack on whatever weed de jour happened to be in her sights.

Then Dad fell ill and eventually died and things began to get on top of her, despite our best efforts to lend a hand. As Mum emerged from her self-imposed purdah she focused on her friends and family, and on getting out and about. Of the house, she said little, but you sensed she was withdrawing from more and more rooms, whittling down her use of the space to her bedroom, the bathroom, kitchen and sitting room. It was understandable, of course. But if she was going to think about the future, and if she was going to make sure she got the most out of it, she didn't need the responsibilities of the house and its once beautiful garden.

We nudged and we nurdled, and tried to get her to think about the family home and the inevitable downsizing. But we drew a blank and were wondering if she would ever grasp the next nettle. Through Easter and the late spring of 2005, we increased the PR campaign, recruiting other members of the family to plant seeds and make suggestions. We got precisely the square root of nowhere. Mum never argued with the logic of a smaller property, or with the need to be realistic about the now five bedrooms of which only one was used regularly. But logic and reason were poor substitutes for memories and her garden. In the end it was the garden that made up her mind. We blitzed it at Easter, the family working as a team, digging out weeds and the encroaching lawns, pruning overgrown shrubs and cutting out the dead and the diseased, but even so it was a superficial attempt to pull nature back. And there was no way we could control Dad's now redundant vegetable patch or maintain his beloved pond. Seeing his little empire choked with weeds, seeing her carefully managed planting becoming unbalanced, hurt her more than any amount of badgering from us.

Finally, some time in the late summer of 2005, I received a call from my mother which went something like this:

'Hello, darling.'

'Hi, Mum, how…'

'Are you free this Saturday?'

'Saturday? I will check but I should be.'

'You'll need to come down on Friday. I need you all day.'

'What…?'

'I've decided to move.'

'Oh, right. So…'

'I've lined up six possibilities. We need to decide.'

'Decide? You've seen them?'

'Of course. Your aunt and I saw them this week.'

'Aunt?' This was the formidable relative, married to Mum's brother, my uncle. She and Mum didn't always see eye-to-eye so it was a surprise to find she had been roped into the hunt for a new home. 'She's in on this, is she?'

'You make it sound like a conspiracy. I merely want to maximise the use of your time. I know how busy you are just now.'

'But, Mum, there's no rush…'

'You and your brother have been nagging me endlessly. You know you are just like your father.'

'Dad?'

'Yes. He was a hypocrite too.'

'Well, yes he was. But how do I fit that mould?'

'Haven't you been bullying me to move since his funeral?'

'It was nagging a moment ago. And all I, all we, have suggested, is that you begin the process…'

'As I said. Just like your father. You may be a skilful lawyer, but your weaselly arguments won't wash. So, are you free?'

'Six properties, you say?'

'Bungalows. In New Milton. We have saved the best to last. So, Saturday. I've told them we will decide, after you've seen them.'

'It sounds like you've made up your mind.'

'Stop it. I can tolerate hypocrisy, but I will not have you whining at me like your father. I value your opinion. When I've heard your thoughts, we can decide.'

I think we both knew she had decided already and I was there because, well because, in a similar situation, Dad would be there, playing the same role as was earmarked for me.

It was a sort of game. I would be expected to try and guess which one she really wanted. If, when put on the spot, I hadn't been astute enough to work out the clues as I went round, then I would receive a look combining withering contempt with a sigh that spoke to the inadequacy of most males to make sensible and informed decisions. Were I to get it right – the social equivalent of panning gold – the proffered look would speak of her pride in how far the effort of teaching us had been worth the effort. I finished work promptly that Friday, collected my bag and car from home, kissed my family goodbye and set off for the New Forest. The sun shone, the traffic was light and I felt a degree of apprehension.

Once again a birthday rhyme, this one from 1990

The Gardener
October 21st, 1990

Barbara's gone into the garden again
(The weeds are in for a shock)
And she'll spend happy hours 'mid her shrubs and her flowers
With never a thought for the clock
*

The October sun is warm on her back
As she works through the herbaceous border,
Green-fingered and sure, coaxing beauty once more
Out of summer's prolific disorder.
*

A drowsy wasp vies with late butterflies
On apples in tumbled profusion,
And there's sweet disarray in the garden today,
A warm, multi-coloured confusion.
*

The old hedge is starred with scarlet rose hips,
Tireless bees plunder each ivy flower.
And where grasses stand tall, unwilling to fall,
Still the cat haunts her summertime bower.
*

Soon clouds will pile high in the dark autumn sky,
And the earth will lie sodden with rain,
Then – in jerkin and boots, not caring two hoots,
Barbs will go gardening again!!!

Ten

Heads You Win...

I think we have established that my mother knows her own mind. I use the present tense, not because I'm a particular believer in the supernatural, but rather because there will forever be a voice in my ear saying 'Geoffrey' – she's one of only two people who use my full name with an annoying regularity (my mother-in-law is the other) – 'don't do that.' Helping her buy a replacement for the family home proved that hypothesis beyond a shadow of a doubt.

They say one of the most stressful things to do is buy a house. It's up there with having a baby, divorce and watching England in the Euros or, indeed, any football tournament. Buying a house with my mother was on the extreme end of that spectrum. The decision had been made to buy first and sell second – at eighty she didn't need the hassle of combining the two moves and, well, you'll see the other reason.

I may have left the impression that Mum was stubborn to the point of intransigence. That was true, but I would have said, before my changed status, that that only applied when it came to what she considered right for her family. For herself, she was, generally, reasonably biddable. Thus, I felt sure that in the case of choosing a new home for herself – the first such purchase in more than thirty-five years, after all – she would listen to reason. Reason being embodied in her lawyerly son. She had developed certain criteria, in consultation with my aunt, which she shared with me:

1. It must have a south or west facing garden.
2. It must be a bungalow.
3. It must be within three roads of New Milton's town centre to help with the shopping trips.
4. It mustn't be completely overlooked.

I thought these sound, if probably in the wrong order. However, in her eyes, she was moving because she couldn't manage her beloved garden; ensuring a suitable, if smaller, replacement was critical. She would need somewhere in which to potter and the last thing she was prepared to tolerate was an east or, worst of all, north facing garden. 'I don't have enough years to cope with that, darling.'

She and my aunt had narrowed down the list to the six we were to visit. I read the details over breakfast. I'll be honest. The first two bungalows appeared pretty unexceptional on paper and I said so.

'You'll need a reference point,' she said, as she refilled my cup, 'and perhaps you'll see something we missed.' This last was said without a trace of irony, though I felt sure she would have been amazed were it to have been true.

We didn't spend long with these controls. One of the two failed spectacularly on point three and the other one on point four though, with this one, the inside was a cosy delight. I could see her there, but when I mentioned this, Mum described it as akin to a priest's hole for the hippy generation. And she thought the owner voted Labour. So that was that.

Number three and four appeared, on paper, more hopeful. Number three had a neat, west facing garden. It appeared not to be overlooked and was clearly within an easy walk of the centre of the town. I mentioned this to her. The non-committal way she offered me more toast told me there was an undisclosed problem, which became all too apparent as soon as we drove up to it an hour or so later.

'Oh right, I see,' I said as I stood by the drive.

'We can't do anything, can we? It isn't something we can change.' Mum looked at me, confident that what we had was a congenital flaw.

The estate agent for this one stood between us. He looked at one of us and then the other, not understanding. He said, 'But it fits each of the criteria, Mrs Le Pard. To the letter.'

I looked at Mum and, together, we said, 'Pebble-dash.'

Dad had this thing about rendered houses, believing the rendering wasn't a decorative feature, but an attempt to hide an architectural wart, incipient dry rot, or subsidence, or just crap construction. It would be disloyal to his memory to take this one forward, however perfect it might otherwise have been.

'But surely you knew, Mrs Le Pard? You've seen this already.' Poor man was stumped why Mum had kept this one on the list.

Mum knew he was trying his best. She decided to point out another flaw, one she was sure he would appreciate. She waved at the front garden and, softening the blow, said, 'They have gnomes too. No, it just wouldn't do.'

What was wrong with number four? The house itself was rather bland though only recently built so came with a string of impressive sounding guarantees. The garden seemed to be something of a movable feast, though. It was still a building site and we were told there were both money and plans in place for a makeover. Which was more than you could say about the fencing. I looked at the proffered plan and tried to make sense of the position of the fence posts and couldn't. 'I don't think this is a good idea, Mum. It looks to me like a dispute in the making.'

She patted my arm. 'I'm glad you said so, darling. I felt there was something wrong and your sage advice settles it. There's also an awful lot of bindweed and you can see the dustbins from the road. Next.'

I'll admit it. Hearing that, I beamed. I might have been a fifty something member of a profession. I might have been a partner for twenty years in an international law firm of some small repute, but Mum taking my advice just then filled me with a warm glow. She was going to listen to me as I had hoped.

Off we headed for numbers five and six, Mum holding tightly onto her stick – she hadn't long had her knee replacement operation. And I allowed myself a little moment imagining how I would help her come to the right decision for her next and final move. The two bungalows left to view were what are known as chalet bungalows which means they aren't bungalows at all but have bedrooms upstairs, built into the slopping roof. In both cases, however, they had plenty of space downstairs if at any stage Mum felt the need to give up on the bedrooms up top. There was a reasonable amount of storage built into what was left of the roof space, the room sizes were decent, the gardens were orientated to the west and, best of all, they both resided on the first residential road after the shops.

All that said, one had been completely refurbished, in beautiful soft tones with the latest equipment and with full regard to the needs of an elderly resident. The other, built in the mid-1970s (they both had in truth), had been lovingly maintained but had had no major work done for at least twenty years. It oozed potential but needed a lot of work. I kept my counsel as we walked round. I asked questions of the agents, I poked and prodded. Mum gave nothing away, chatting to the owners, admiring some feature here, some picture there.

We thanked the last agent for his time and withdrew back home to consider what we had seen. I was offered tea and crumpets.

'Well, darling?'

'Well, Mum. The first one was immaculate. You may want to change the odd piece of wallpaper, but it is ready to move in. Not all of it would be your taste…'

'Oh no, I think it is lovely.'

Was that a clue? Or a trap? Hmm.

'The other is just perfect for someone who wants a blank canvas to create their own home. It looks tired, but someone could make a lot of it. That said such a person would be committing to a heck of a lot of work.'

'Oh yes. Six months probably.'

'Yes. At least. Walls to take out, plumbing changes, new boiler, a completely new kitchen and windows and so on.'

'What about price?'

'I don't think that is too much of an issue. The difference would cover the cost of the refurbishment. But you would have to manage the builders. You couldn't live there. It would need daily visits to check up. A lot to manage. Maybe you should sleep on it.'

'We will put an offer in on Monday.'

'Mum. That's a bit soon. Shouldn't we…?'

'Darling, which one?'

I studied that seemingly bland countenance, the inexpressive eyes, the static eyebrows, the gentle curve of her mouth, suggesting a smile somewhere nearby.

'Logic and good sense says a woman entering her eighties with a dodgy knee, arthritis and eye sight that has seen better days, should go for the finished product. However, you want to do the doey-uppey, don't you?'

'Should I?'

'Do you want my opinion?'

'Yes.'

'Will you listen to it?'

'If it accords with my own, yes.'

'And if not?'

'I have spent nearly fifty-five years, apparently moderating my views to allow your father to think he was in charge of the big decisions and I'm not wasting time training you up only for you to let me down. I need reinforcement, not resistance.'

'Ok. I guessed as much. Well, let's have some fun then. You'll need to stay here, won't you?' "Here" being the family home.

She beamed. She had me just where she wanted me. 'Mum, when I gave you that legal advice, on house number four, about the fence. If you had wanted that bungalow, would you have listened to me?'

She smiled. Mum could really unleash a smile when she wanted to. 'I don't think we need to consider speculative what-ifs, do we? Do we offer the asking price or go for a negotiation?'

We took a walk that afternoon, along the cliffs at Barton. When we moved to Hampshire, in the winter of 1969/70, it was the first walk we took, in the wind and spitting drizzle. Dad spent most of it worried that our dog, a boxer called Punch, would take it into its head that he had some lemming ancestry and start a mad rush for the edge. While he called to Punch to 'Come back, boy,' he waved vaguely at the clouds that had removed the view and said, 'over there is the Isle of Wight.' We took it on trust. But that day, with Mum, the sky was clear and the view sharp. Dad loved visiting the Island, on one of his many bug hunts. This poem of his was inspired by one such journey across the narrow straits from Lymington to Yarmouth. We did it every year in the spring, to the southern undercliff, to check up on the health of a colony of Marsh Fritillary butterflies. In memory, it was always fine.

Island Ferry

Crisp and fresh is the air this morning on the open upper deck
While the muddy river waters froth and churn,
There's a drift of salty spray as our vessel pulls away,
And Lymington is slowly left astern.
*

The sun is still half-hidden in the early morning haze,
And all around the screaming seagulls fly,
And, ahead, the Island lies on a barely seen horizon
Like a supine giant, dark against the sky.
*

Across the gleaming mudflats the distant reedbeds stand,
A verdant carpet, lavishly unrolled,
While beyond, the tops of trees, barely stirring in the breeze,
Catch the morning sun and briefly glow with gold.
*

A solitary heron, still and silent, sees us pass,
Poised to strike and single-minded, shows no fear,
For the swirling tide reveals the writhing, silver eels,
And swiftly falls that deadly darting spear.
*

Past the Yacht Club and Marina, past a multitude of masts,
Past the posts and buoys that mark our course along,
'Till the Solent is before us and seabirds' raucous chorus

Is mingled with the rising sea-wind song.

*

The mist has nearly gone now, and across a sparkling sea
The Ferry, slow and steady, makes her way,
And all the world is bright in the shining morning light,
With the promise of a lovely summer's day.

Eleven

Restoration Woman

Mum continued to do things her way. In the autumn of 2005, she met with her trusty builder, Roger Torah, to plan what needed doing. The place was tired, 1970s tired, which frankly wasn't a decade the aesthetic from which you felt inclined to try to preserve; as seems to be the case today in trendy cafes, one can have too much avocado.

But any idea I might have had that she wanted a tidy up plus a few new appliances was scotched on Roger's first visit. First up, my train was late getting in so Mum and Roger were already engaged on a detailed debate when I walked through the door. I didn't need to hear the words. I just had to see him tapping walls to know we were talking structural, not superficial.

'Your mum seems to think knocking through here and extending the kitchen is a good idea.'

She didn't meet my eye. I smiled at him. 'Oh yes. I think it is essential.'

She beamed at me. Craven. Coward. Quisling. I could hear the Textiliste and my sister in law ready to point out why such extensive works were unnecessary.

Perhaps a slight backtrack is needed. Like a lot of rural homes circa 1965 to 1985, the advent of central heating hadn't changed the attitude that you didn't just heat everywhere. Oh no. You turned on radiators in bedrooms (a) if there was a sign of damp (b) if guests were due (c) if advised by at least two medical professionals that your child's life depended on it. You certainly did not do so because a child complained about the ice on the inside of the windowpane.

As a consequence, the one room where you might always find someone was the kitchen, filled with steam – not always pleasant steam: boiled handkerchiefs are not in the same olfactory ballpark as vanilla pods and crusty white bread. But steam is begat by warmth.

We now have a little wooden sign on our kitchen wall that we inherited from Mum: *No matter where I place my guests, they always like my kitchen best* (alongside: *If it's not one thing, it's your mother* which is another memoir entirely). It summed up life with my parents and Mum was never happier than when in her kitchen.

47

Therefore, creating the perfect kitchen was, to me, as essential as making sure the toilets flushed.

Mum waxed lyrically about Bessemer beams and supporting columns; the best place for the sink and... She stopped. 'Come with me.' This was, I guessed, aimed at both of us.

She was on a roll, the sort of roll that stones embark upon when intent on gathering no naysayers. Off the narrow hallway, just outside the kitchen, sat two cupboards full of bits of carpet kindly left by the previous owner in the expectation that purple and cerise onion swirls made from a polyester and Brillo mix would one day reinvent themselves as the must-have floor covering. Mum opened the one to the right. 'Imagine,' Mum didn't use words like imagine – not practical enough, 'a toilet.'

I breathed again. A downstairs loo wasn't a bad idea. I did think I should add a note of caution. 'There's a bathroom behind here, Mum. You don't need another toilet, do you?'

Mum was of the school that considered an extra toilet in the same way a starving dog considers a rotisserie chicken. Gift horses were never so dentally ignored as when they comprised a toilet. 'I have plans.'

Gradually Mum unveiled these plans. They translated into a quote of fourteen pages in length. In amongst the basics there were: a gravel drive replacing tarmac ('I've always wanted to have a crunch when I drive up to the house' by which I understood her to mean creating a sound like waves on a beach through slow moving tyres driven across the pebbles and not that she planned on eliminating the neighbours' cat); an electronic door to the garage; and a car port to keep her dry as she unloaded her shopping. These were all features which Dad would not have countenanced believing them to be "too namby-pamby" or "too snobby".

In truth, some of them were barely even practical, which wasn't exactly what one expected of Mum. When, later, someone pointed this out, she said, 'Exactly.' Was she really such a changed woman?

While she focused on the house I began clearing the new garden. Most of it was lawn, but about two thirds of the way back there was a line of trees and shrubs that gave the garden some character. Mum loved this mature border; it wasn't her usual mix, but I set about de-weeding it and making the whole thing presentable, ready for when she would be ready to start to potter.

While I was working on it a neighbour leant over the fence and introduced himself. He saw Mum with Roger, the ever-present tape measure in his hand. 'Your mum's got plans then.'

Yes. Plans. I smiled and nodded. Plans meant she was looking forward. Plans meant she was keeping busy. Plans were good.

Roger was excellent; I think he enjoyed working with Mum. She demanded high standards, but she wasn't silly. She made quick and sensible decisions (building decisions, that is; the cost wasn't a factor high on her list – I made it clear she should not worry about cost until we knew the extent of what she wanted and then we could whittle if necessary – not that we did) and he made sensible suggestions, accommodating her age and physical limitations in a sensitive way. But even so, my plan to have her moved in before the winter proved well short of the mark. And we had agreed she would only move when it was completely ready and we would only sell the family house once she was in.

Finally, in the early months of 2006, the end was in sight. It looked fantastic. Everything was ready. All we had to do was pack up her home of the last thirty-seven years, move five miles down the road to a house half the size, and sell the family manor. Easy-peasy.

Not.

Mum and Dad came across Roger Torah and his men in the last years of the Twentieth Century as they planned and executed a house extension they'd wanted for years. They delighted in every aspect of it, even happily living in crazy conditions while the roof was off and the gales blew – well, Mum did. This birthday poem reflects on that time and, well, during the refurbishment of her bungalow I saw some of what Dad describes here.

Industrial Partnership
October 21 2000

When workmen descended on Silver Crest
And started in with incredible zest
Demolishing walls and digging up floors
Removing windows and taking out doors
I was frightened to death, of course, because
I panic.
*

Barbara, however, had none of my qualms
And welcomed them with open arms
(Obviously longing to interchange roles
They do the watching while she digs the holes!)
And considered their efforts with scaffolding poles
Titanic.
*

She knew from the start that I'd get the hump
And briskly told me, 'Now don't be a chump,'
'Take a positive view and be like me'
'Cos it's all going to be such fun, you'll see'
'And if you don't see you can make the tea'
Decisive.
*

She spoke with considerable expertise
Of the relative merits of those bits and these
And discussed with the plumber the site of the loo
Had chats with brickies, the hod carrier too
While I stood around not having a clue
Derisive.
*

The extent of her knowledge was plain to see
And impressed everybody, especially me,
She knew what she wanted and where it should go
This room or that, up high or down low
She stuck to her guns and wouldn't take no
Emphatic.
*

When a new worker appeared on site
And asked a question I quivered in fright
And waffled and muttered in desperation
Broke out all over in cold perspiration
But Barbara soon rescued the situation
Diplomatic.
*

At meetings on site I don't say a lot
Knowing Barbara will always know what's what
For it's no good asking me what's planned
Technical matters I just don't understand
So thank God she's there to hold my hand.
GUESS WHO???

Twelve

Strategizing

The months rolled forward and summer approached. The builders were planning to hand over in mid-April so a move in early May, or maybe June, was realistic. I felt we could now plan the move in some detail and sort out the sale – Mum was adamant she wanted to move only when we had the sale fixed. I remained hopeful the two events might happen in fairly close order.

Mum was sanguine about the prospect of the move; she had already moved emotionally, and she enjoyed each final season with a slightly melancholic relish, rubbing eucalypt leaves between her fingers and collecting seeds from fritillaria and foxglove to add to her new flower beds.

The contorted willow, one of her many successes, began to bud as we planned the move, its deep olive-green leaves a reminder of one of Dad's many rootless anxieties. 'You remember his panic when I said I wanted a willow here,' she said, her gaze far into the distance as she spoke. 'Silly man. Just imagine the state he'd be in now (with a move to plan).'

The panic was the result of twenty years of guilt over an illegal overflow from our cesspit. Dad knew of the overflow, from the day they bought the house back in 1969, and I think he knew it didn't exactly comply with the relevant regulations from about that time too, not that he ever acknowledged that fact.

What he couldn't do was pretend he didn't know it was there. In dry summers, indeed, in any dry spell, when what passed for a lawn turned a mottled beige, the verdant green strip that ran diagonally across it from behind the sheds to the hedge that abutted Barrows Lane was like a punk rocker who had experimented with a green Mohican astride his otherwise blond locks and rather gave away that there was something strange going on. And it was hardly surprising when you realised that every time someone had a bath, diluted faecal matter would seep from the seventy-year-old overflow pipe before spilling into the ditch.

We both smiled at the memory. We could hear that voice, slightly squeaky when under stress, like he needed oiling. 'Barbs, the willow finds water. It'll be inside that – you know where – like a ferret up the trousers and if the council gets wind…'

'Don't be ridiculous, darling.' Mum's put downs always comprised a mix of infantilising the speaker with a leavening of love. 'It'll not happen.'

'What if it breaks the pipe? What if...?'

'Don't worry.'

But he did. As he had already been doing for years. The tree went in one birthday and Dad waited for disaster. It did come, finally, in the late 1990s when a combination of a lorry driving into the ditch, when trying to let another lorry pass, and a steamy hot summer led to the council "getting wind" in a very tangible way.

'Did you know you have an illegal overflow, mate?' The council official had been inspecting the damage to see what needed to be done to repair the ditch – without free-flowing ditches the flooding in winter could do a lot of damage, not that they often worried about such things.

He had come round to the garden and found Dad trying not to appear as if he was watching what was going on.

'Really? That's appalling.' Dad was an enthusiastic if erratic liar, but he pulled this one off with a straight face. 'The previous owners never said.' He omitted to mention he had lived in the house for over twenty-five years at this point. 'I'll get it sorted at once.'

The official was understanding and left Dad to it. He might have forgotten, but Dad wasn't going to take a chance. Partly we - the Archaeologist and I – felt cheated, since Dad's regular panics when anyone official visited generated much amusement. But really it was because we had been calling for this to be sorted for years. As children, growing up, we were very aware of the smell on hot summer days.

And that wasn't the worst of it. An old-fashioned cesspit needs to be emptied; the modern alternative, the septic tank, does too. The difference is in the method. The cesspit is opened, and pumped out; the septic tank, has a hose fitted to the top and is sucked out. One generates a smell that English adjectives are inadequate to describe; the other is mildly unpleasant if you get too close.

The occasions when "Lavender" Jim came to empty the cesspit were legendary. One has to assume that this burly, jolly man with his toothy smile and indescribably coloured overalls – Dulux has never sought to replicate that particular shade - had zero sense of smell. While Mum hurried round closing all windows and doors, we boys would make ourselves scarce – say France or at least the woods down the lane - as he pumped and bucketed it empty. We both made a mental note deleting another career choice off our list.

The modern septic tank that replaced our cesspit sat buried next to his greenhouses. Both Mum and I turned to look at them and sighed together. His greenhouses were Dad's place of refuge, where he could compose poetry or get his thoughts straight when feeling overwhelmed. Seeing them then, neglected and unkempt, brought home as nothing else did how far the garden had deteriorated.

'Come on, Mum. Let's make tea and plan this move.'

Here is another birthday poem, which epitomises Dad's romantic side and his deep, enduring love for his beloved Barbs; some of you will note the different style used by Dad for the date in the poem's heading – if only he had been consistent!

21/10/88

Warm and gently you always have been
Unkindness in you has no place
And whatever you do your nature shines through
For you have a laughing face.
The years that have gone have been good to me
With problems, thank God, mostly small
But however I tried, without you by my side
I wouldn't have coped at all.
For you make the dark days bright, my love,
And my troubles you soothe away
Life's just begun! It's going to be fun!
Many happy returns of the day!!

Thirteen

Particulars

As the building works progressed, Mum became more determined only to move when she knew the family house had been sold. She had a point; I've been told more than once that it is easier to sell a home (not a new home but a used one that would need work) that is warm and cosy and lived in – so long as it isn't a mess or smelly – than a tired, empty one. The details of the move, therefore, went on hold while we sorted out the sale.

Mum may have reached a settled intention to move, but it was different for my children and the Archaeologist's. They were devastated at the idea of the sale. Grandma and Grandpa's house was a very tangible part of their upbringing, a place of the happiest of memories. I understood and explained why Mum needed somewhere smaller.

'But why sell? Why don't you buy it off her and let it? Then we can use it in the future.'

Leaving aside it made no sense, I had none of the emotional connections they had. Sure, it would always be a part of me, my history, but "home" has never been a place for me, not really; it's more a state of mind. Maybe when they have lived in as many different flats and houses as I have they will feel differently. In a way though, I envied them that umbilical linkage; it had to make the memories sharper, deeper, didn't it?

Time slipped and it wasn't until late June that I visited Mum as we had an appointment with, reputedly, the best estate agents in Lymington. That turned out to be something of a misnomer, but we didn't know it at the time. More to the point, we had no expectations on how attractive the house would be.

Mum and Dad bought it in 1969 for six thousand five hundred pounds. Since then, they extended it in several ways. If somewhat lacking when built, it was, by 2006, a well-proportioned, five bedroomed "cottage", sitting inside the boundary of the New Forest National Park and, of course, with its fabulous garden. It was surrounded by farms and another ten houses or so but otherwise resided in rural isolation.

This isolation was real; there was no public transport, the nearest shop was well over a mile away and the road past the front of the house wasn't labelled the "Lymington Grand Prix" for no reason. It was a corner plot with one boundary facing a quiet side road leading towards the Forest proper and the village of Sway two and a bit miles away. The junction was dreadful though, and in the thirty-seven years there, there had been numerous accidents, including at least one fatality.

'Oooo,' he said, he being the agent we spoke to. 'Where exactly?' He was dribbling, metaphorically, as he imagined the fee. 'Circa four hundred and fifty thousand pounds, I'd say. Obviously, I'll need to check.'

Mum nodded, I smiled. We were both rather stunned.

'We should put it on at four hundred and seventy-five. Perfect time, too.'

'Why?' we both asked together. We weren't capable of anything other than to query the timing.

'Start of the school hols in a week or so. Loads of people come here for a break, fall in love and decide to buy somewhere. This is ideal.'

Mum and I exchanged another smile, congratulating each other on our foresight in delaying the sale to this point.

The man – Mr Gubbins, perhaps, he seemed to be a Gubbins – began to scribble. It became apparent that he was determined to launch the property on this gullible audience and would do all in his power to ensure it coincided with the said holidays. That allowed roughly two weeks to sort all the necessary admin. 'I'll have someone come and take pictures,' he rifled through his desk, I assume after a diary, 'and I'll need to see your home and draft some particulars so…' More frowns, then a smile as he found the diary; it was a genetically enhanced smile that added significantly to global warming, 'Shall we say I get the draft to you on…' He reeled off a date.

I checked my calendar. Problem number one.

'We're both going away – a residential course in Marlborough - for a week. Maybe we could launch when we get back. That way we can make sure everything is just so.'

Gubbins was not happy; his smile-come-dribble became a pout and from the new criss-cross of lines on his forehead, it appeared his haemorrhoids were making an unscheduled and unwelcome reappearance. 'If you leave us the keys we can show people round.'

Now both of us weren't happy. Mum didn't like leaving keys with this man – he had called her Barbara which was assuming a level of redundant intimacy with which she did not approve - and I wanted to know the particulars were done correctly before they were let loose; I also wanted a survey done, to be offered to a potential buyer so they truly bought as was.

Gubbins, however, hadn't spent years making Faustian pacts with all and sundry in order to secure a commission. He knew which buttons to press.

'Mrs Le Pard,' credit points there for recognising her preferred mode of address without being told, 'I assure you no one in the squillion years we have been serving ladies such as yourself has ever had cause to worry if we hold the keys.'

He affected a coyness unbecoming in one so patently rapacious. 'Do you know Willow Cottage on Vaggs Lane?'

Of course, she did. It was previously owned by one of the Valkyries who ran the Hordle Women's Institute. He read my mother like a well-thumbed book. 'Margaret's place?'

'We sold it for her last year. She was delighted with our service and we held the keys for her. Please. Ask her. I know she will be happy to confirm.'

Mum allowed herself to be persuaded – generally she didn't fall for the charms of snake oil salespeople, but Gubbins must have had a secret musk undetectable to fifty something male lawyers.

He turned to me, sure, I suppose, that Mum would not ask Margaret for fear of seeming incapable of making up her own mind – the perils of independent womanhood in Mum's generation can be the assumptions they carry around about how they should behave; another insidious treachery perpetrated by the patriarchy.

'Geoff, I will not show the house to anyone without your say so. But, you have an email account?'

I nodded. He made it sound new-fangled. Was he trying to flatter me by suggesting I would be up with all things "modern"?

'I will send you the draft. I would welcome all help perfecting the particulars. I'm sure you'll be able to polish the, erm…?' He glanced at Mum, possibly unsure where to take his metaphor.

'Turd,' she helped him without hesitation.

He rocked back a little but rallied well. 'Yes, I was thinking "prose", but that about covers it, I'm sure.'

Gubbins agreed to produce the draft particulars for our approval and, assuming they passed the test, show people around. He called it a "pre-look", if the particulars hadn't been printed. But he was keen - as were we, in truth – to get the ball rolling.

Gubbins wasn't bad at what he did. I planned on collecting Mum on the Saturday to take her to Marlborough – we were to meet the Textiliste there to participate in their fabulous summer school – and in the week before, he did as he promised: visiting and swooning over the house and garden; having a photographer take some lovely snaps; arranging for someone to measure; and pulling together some part-way decent particulars. When he collected the keys on the Friday, I think it is fair to say Mum and I were both content.

The one small fly in the ointment was the seller's survey.

If you are reading this and are unfamiliar with the English way of selling a house, then let me just say it is not fit for purpose and a shambles.

However, one way to mitigate some of the pain is to do a lot of good preparatory work, one piece being to provide any prospective buyer with a survey that sets out, warts and all, the current condition of the house. You might think it best to try and hide the faults, but if you have experienced the trauma of nearly signing a contract to sell, only to have some unscrupulous scumbag of a buyer reveal a dodgy survey and blackmail you, with either a price chip or they pull out, you will understand why I wanted to avoid that trap.

We wanted a speedy, and pain-free sale. The house, while in pretty good nick, had its issues and a survey would mean the buyer knew and factored them into his or her price.

Gubbins understood; this was going to be an easy sell, he indicated so the buyers would be lining up and prepared to accept the challenges shown by any survey without significant reductions in price.

The chosen surveyor visited and told me what he had found – a few issues which were the sort to lead to minor but irritating quibbles - but, by the time I picked Mum up, he had yet to type up the report. 'Fear not, Mr Le Pard. I'll have it with Mr Gubbins by Tuesday, latest.' I believed him. I usually do, being the trusting sort.

As we filled up the boot with Mum's bag for the week, who should pull into her drive in his large Merc but Gubbins.

He was all sharp suit and atomic smile.

The sky was cerulean, the temperature just a shade off balmy. 'Good day for it.' "It" was unspecified, but I assumed selling houses featured highly. 'I usually come this way and when I saw you, I just had to stop. I just wanted to assure you that we will look after your home in your absence.'

I don't think he bowed to Mum, but it felt as if he might have.

We exchanged what are known as pleasantries. Well, I did. Mum made a show of climbing into the passenger seat and strapping herself in. When he had gone and I had double-checked everything was locked up and settled in the driver's seat, Mum looked at me. 'What do you think of that young man?' she asked.

'I guess he'll do a good job.'

She patted down her trousers and nodded, rubbing at her new knee which had not yet fully mobilised. 'Yes, I suppose. It's just a shame he is such a prick.'

In the 1970s a television programme called That's Life hit the TV screens. It was part consumer complaints show and part jokey reality TV based on subjects and stories supplied by the viewing public. One of the regular presenters was an ancient comic called Cyril Fletcher who penned his Odd Odes, long poems that had the taint of the music hall about them. Dad enjoyed them, it's true, but really he knew he could do better. This is his…

An E-loo-sive Tale

This is the tale of Pamela Way
Who, on a shopping trip one day
Discovered that she wanted to
Pay a visit to the loo.
Trouble was she didn't know
Down which street she ought to go.
So, she thought 'I'll ask a local
Passing girl – if not, a bloke'll
Point the way if he is kind
To where I can find peace of mind.'
Alas, alack, 'twas not to be,
They all were strangers there, you see,
And none of them had any clue
Where she could find the local loo.
Mind you, they tried, without a doubt,
They even hailed a passing Scout
Who had a knife and rope with toggle,
And a quite enormous woggle.
He said, 'I'll soon stop this rumpus'.
And from his shorts produced a compass.
But sad to say, his poor technique
Left Pam still squirming, so to speak.
Another chap who did his best
Wore Y-fronts and a pink string vest.
(When someone rudely asked him, 'Why?'
He said, 'I haven't got a tie!')
But, although his dress was odd,
He was a most resourceful bod
And from his vest pulled out a map

And spread it flat upon his lap.
But this, too, was no good at all
The scale, I fear, was far too small
And didn't show a single loo
(which upset our poor you-know-who)
She bravely smiled – 'Nil Desperandum'
And simply chose a street at random.
Then gazed around with eager eye
But not a loo could she spy,
Until, beyond a broken fence
She saw a notice – 'Ladies/gents'!
Nothing now could hold her back
And, like a runner on a track
She forward sprang as if by magic,
Then stopped, aghast – Oh God, how tragic!
Another notice barred her way
Which read 'These loos are closed today.'
Poor Pamela, complete frustration
Made her weep with desperation.
Then as she sobbed, her bitter tears
Woke her up! Hurrah! Three Cheers!
For it had been a dream, you see,
And so, she laughed with joy and glee,
And, casting off all thoughts of gloom,
Rushed, happy into the bathroom.

Fourteen

A Sale, A Sale (Part One)

We left for Marlborough College in Mum's Peugeot 205, with me driving. The plan was to meet the Textiliste in Marlborough for a cream tea – the Polly Tea Rooms have always been a favourite – after which we would register for our courses and obtain access to our accommodation. Mum was doing découpage and mosaics, the Textiliste printing, and I was mixing a morning of outdoor adventures with an afternoon of poetry appreciation. I had even hired a collapsible wheelchair in case Mum's knee wasn't up to the distances you needed to walk between classrooms. It was a godsend, as it turned out.

We had hardly gone ten miles when my phone rang. Not having hands free, it meant pulling in. I left it for another half an hour and then stopped for some comfort, always welcome, and to check. I imagined it was the Textiliste updating us on her journey.

It was Gubbins. He sounded dizzy with excitement. Very perky indeed. 'I didn't want to say earlier, because I needed to check the appointment book, but the early birders are pecking, Mr Le Pard. Geoff.'

A forlorn sparrow scratched without enthusiasm at the service station tarmac, a counterpoint to Gubbins' enthusiasm. 'We've managed to line up a couple of visits for later today, from those who have already registered an interest…'

'But the particulars won't be ready until Tuesday, you said. I understood that was when…'

He ho-ho-hoed. Like a donkey-Santa cross. 'Mr Le Pard, Geoffrey, Geoff, paperwork, just paperwork. They are begging for a view.' I could imagine him standing out front, waving towards the house. 'It sells itself; you don't need room sizes and carpets included for this one to go. Anyway, I'll let them have a photocopy of the draft and, if they like it, I'll send them the final version when it is done.'

I needed something to curtail his boyish enthusiasm, as a little birdie twittered "more haste, less speed" into my ear. 'Don't forget to tell them about the survey.'

'Of course. And when will that be ready?'

I had already told him but repeated what I had said.

'If anyone shows an interest, Mr Le Pard, I'll be sure to pass it on.'

'Make sure they know they are bidding, taking into account…'

'I think you can rest assured…'

I zoned out and cut the call. Mum suggested a coffee. As we made our way, gingerly in her case, to the seating, she said, 'I'm sure Mr Gubbins knows how to organise a sale, darling. It's why his fees are so astronomical.'

Another birthday poem

(21/10/92)

Barbara's gone into the garden again
Like she has done so often before
I know I'm not wrong 'cos her anorak's gone
And her slippers are by the back-door.
*

I knew when we woke on this cool autumn day
With hardly a cloud in the sky
And the whole world sun-kissed, that she'd never resist
And would soon wave dull housework goodbye.
*

Look thro' the French windows – see, there she is now
With her barrow loaded with tools
Where the October sun glows on a climbing pink rose
And late daisies still glimmer like jewels.
*

A robin is watching her every move
And now hungrily, hopefully lingers
And she kneels, trowel in hand, where bright dahlias stand
Untouched, as yet, by frosty fingers.
*

She makes things grow where none grew before
(Unlike me, her failures are few)
For the plants that she tends she loves like old friends
And, like us, I think they love her, too.
*

Barbara's gone into the garden again
And there she will busily stay
'Midst her flowers and shrubs and plant pots and tubs
And be happy the livelong day.
*

And when, all too soon, winter takes bitter hold
And lowering skies threaten snow
While we shiver and whinge and by fireside cringe
We all know where Barbara will go!!

Fifteen

A Sale, A Sale (Part Two)

During that summer of 2006, an overcast humid July from memory, Marlborough seemed like an oasis. The summer school comprises so many classes it rather blows the mind. When we arrived, we were greeted by the sight of a complicated dry-stone wall snaking its way across the grass; in another corner there was a sand-carved Harry Potteresque sculpture. We wheeled Mum around to see the place and had a lovely dinner. Mum and the Textiliste enjoyed a Pimm's and we listened to a jazz band as the sun set over Wiltshire. Perfect.

Sunday was a slow day, but on the Monday morning I was to learn how to kayak. To begin with I headed for the swimming pool and still water; frankly, I hated it. I'm not keen on water deeper than my knees and the idea that I was to maintain stability using my thighs brought on cramp and a feeling that staying in the office would have been preferable. By the time I had dried off and dressed for lunch, I needed to run to Mum's workrooms. Of course, she was placed in the furthest part of the college. Every day I had to sprint to try and make sure Mum was on time for the food. While I huffed and puffed Mum enjoyed the ride.

It wasn't until we sat down that I checked my Blackberry. I had tried to admit I didn't need to check, that it wasn't any sort of addiction, but the truth was I felt compelled. I could make easy excuses about the office needing me, but this was a holiday and I knew I should be more grown-up.

So, here I was, somewhat stressed about the water, annoyed I had signed up to something I should have realised I wouldn't enjoy, sweaty from the wheelchair grand prix and guilty that I was giving in to an urge I should have been able to fight.

There was a text message from an unknown mobile asking me to call. It had to be work, a colleague maybe who needed my help – of course only I could help, so big was my ego. But it wasn't so big that I dared calling in front of the Textiliste. I waited until after lunch and I had deposited Mum before I rang the number as I jogged towards poetry. It was Gubbins. Oh dear, what had gone wrong?

'Good news, Mr Le Pard. We've had an offer. Two actually.'

'Blimey.'

'The highest is thirty thousand below the asking price and the buyer is in a long chain.'

'I'll tell Mum.'

'My advice is to wait. We've had six viewings…'

'Six?'

'And three second viewings.'

'Are the details out yet?'

'Wednesday. Not that anyone cares. I've lined up two more first viewings today and three more for later in the week. We can certainly do better than the current offers.'

'You will mention the survey? I…'

'Must dash. Another call.'

After a dabble with John Donne and Milton, I skipped my way to the workroom, in my head praising Le Gubbins.

Mum was delighted. When I told her I had agreed to reject the underbid she smiled and touched my hand. 'I'll leave all that up to you, darling. I know you'll do the best job. Mr Gubbins is good, isn't he?'

I didn't comment. From prick to prince in a weekend. Whatever next?

Tuesday and I was mountain biking. This I enjoyed, but we were late back so once again I was running hither and yon to get Mum to and from lunch. But I checked the phone as soon as I could. Sure enough, Gubbins had called again.

'The particulars are out, a day early. They look rather magnificent, though I say it myself. And a single lady, who has just retired, is really keen. She's gone in at five thousand under, but I'm sure we can push her up.'

'Did you tell her about the survey? I called the surveyor and you will have the final version soon.'

'Mr Le Pard, shall we secure a sale first?'

'Yes, but this is important…'

'Good. We will ensure everything is in order. So, we hold out?'

I left him to it, but that afternoon as the class pondered the beauty of Keats' sonnets and Wordsworth's trite rhymes, I began to want to strangle Gubbins. He was so bloody smug. Then my phone went off in the class and I suffered instant death by tutor-glare as I fumbled to turn it off. I could see it was Gubbins.

I called as soon as we finished, on my way to pick up Mum. 'Mrs Wotsit has agreed to the asking price. Mr and Mrs Thingy are seeing it again today. And we have three more first views later this week as well as several potentials at the weekend. I wondered what you wanted to do.'

'That's a lot of interest. Have you told them we have received the asking price?'

'I will. After all, we've barely started, Mr Le Pard. I'd say, if you were so minded, we could give it, say, another week to ten days and go to best bids. The market is hot hot hot. You may even make five hundred thousand.'

I began to like Gubbins. He was transparently self-interested. It felt like I could hear his brain calculating his fee at every level of asking price, like a committed darts player who, despite no ability at maths, can still subtract any number from five hundred and one in micro-seconds. 'I'll talk to Mum, but that sounds like a good idea to me. And the survey…'

'Mr Le Pard, I'll let them know when I get it…'

'Ok. It is…'

'Yes, you said.'

Maybe I was being a touch paranoid and I should have been focusing on the sale. After all, if the property was so popular, maybe I shouldn't stress so.

Mum was a bit tired after a tough afternoon making mosaics so I left things until dinner. Over a pre-dinner Pimm's things went in an unexpected direction.

'I spoke to Gubbins.'

'He is a nice man. Though the braces do him no favours.'

'Yes, well, he tells me a Mrs Wotsit – she's single and there's no chain or need for a mortgage - has offered the asking price and…'

'Oh, how marvellous. After just three days. Mr Gubbins is good, isn't he?' She turned to my wife. 'Rather full of himself and inclined to BT.'

The Textiliste nodded, but I was confused. 'BT? The telephone people?'

'You young people say it. It was on Emmerdale. Making things up.'

I think the Textiliste liked the "young people". 'I think you mean BS, Barbs.'

'Of course. Silly me. Bull spit.'

I didn't correct her. 'Well, arguably he's behind the market.'

Mum rattled her ice cubes. 'I think that is a rather churlish thing to say.'

'Mum, your house is gold just now. Everyone loves it…'

'Your father would be pleased.'

'Of course. The thing is, he suggested an asking price of four hundred and seventy-five thousand and it's clearly worth a lot more. There are several people still interested…'

'Well, of course we don't want to disappoint anyone, but, well, that's just the way it is, I suppose. We could have told him to put it higher.'

'That's his job. Anyway, it doesn't really matter.'

'No, of course it doesn't. We are where we are.'

'Quite. So, the thing is, we can go to best bids…'

The smile that had reappeared slipped a little. Not a good sign. 'What are "best bids", darling?' This was said in the same voice she used if I came home covered in something I hadn't gone out in. As in "what is that on your shirt/shoes/trousers/pullover/face?"

'We wait until everyone has expressed an interest and we ask them to put in their best price, into a sealed envelope and then we open them all and the top bid wins.'

'But why do that when we have the asking price? All they'll do is put in the asking price.'

'No, that's the beauty, Mum, they go above the asking price.'

I had truly farted in front of royalty, while asking Mum if her cake was shop bought. She couldn't have looked more horrified. 'You can't do that.'

'Why not?'

'Because we asked for a price and now you're asking for another one.'

'But there's nothing to stop us.'

'There's nothing stopping Sainsbury's trying to raise the price of their own brand baked beans when I reach the till – not that I buy them because they reduce the salt – but they just don't. I'd have to go to Tesco if they did.'

'Mum, we aren't worried about brand loyalty.'

'I'm worried about your moral compass. You're not becoming one of those awful impregnators, are you?'

'Do you mean entrepreneurs?'

'Don't be clever. Your father would be horrified at how your standards have slipped. Best bibs, indeed.'

'Bids.'

'Mrs Wotsit won fair and square. We sell to her.' Mum looked away. The argument was over. There was no need for a moderator. The "I'll leave it to you, darling" was a short lived but oft repeated example of how parental flattery could be used to keep me on track until such time as what I was doing conflicted with what Mum wanted. We accepted the asking price.

I was miffed. The Textiliste understood but shrugged. She wouldn't have told Mum. She knew which way the conversation would go. And I forgot the survey until the Friday when Gubbins called to confirm Mrs Wotsit had instructed her lawyers.

'The survey? Have you given it to Mrs Wotsit?'

'Survey?'

'Mr Gubbins…'

'I haven't seen it.'

'The surveyor said he delivered a set of six copies yesterday.'

'I will check and pass it on.'

'Mrs Wotsit needs to understand her bid assumes she has read and accepted the results.'

'She's getting her own done.'

'Yes, exactly.'

'I will deal with it. You enjoy your holiday.'

He didn't. He sent all the copies to Mum's solicitor who passed one on without comment. Six weeks later the solicitor called me to say Mrs Wotsit wanted my reaction to their survey results. 'Are her points in our survey as well?'

She checked. 'Yes, all there.'

'Tell her, that her bid was based on her accepting the property as seen and as revealed by our survey.'

She came back. 'That wasn't her understanding.'

I knew it. I bloody knew it. I didn't tell Mum, but I did call Gubbins. He blamed the solicitor who blamed him.

'You know what, Mr Gubbins, I really don't care. We will lose the sale, but we will not be chiselled. Not one penny.'

He huffed, he puffed. I think he had another go at the solicitor. In the end both reduced their fees by the amount of the chiselling.

I still wish we had gone to best bids though.

As with his Paratrooper's Prayer I shared earlier, this was written by Dad when in his teens, around his eighteenth birthday, before he was posted to Palestine.

Tommy

He was young but weep not for Tommy
Who is resting now, at peace
He knew joys in life and a little strife
And now, The Great Release.
As a soldier his job was war
His tools a bayonet and gun
And sometimes they frowned and wondered
How wildly he took his fun.
He has lived, so weep not for Tommy
But smile, and remember with pride
How, taught to kill, he loved to live
And took with both hands all this world would give
And how, like a man, he died.

Sixteen

Needing TARDIS

Now that we had a buyer for Mum's house, we needed to plan the move. The building works on her bungalow were all done as were the legal details on the sale. 'When do you want to move, Mum? We should set the time frame.'

That's me, ever the lawyer, trying to get one up in the negotiations.

'Well, I spoke to Mrs Gerund (our buyer – Mrs Wotsit was made up; so is Mrs Gerund – I simply cannot remember her name) and she's keen on moving in the first week of September.'

We need a pause here. First, I didn't know Mum and Mrs Gerund were in touch. I'd have tried to put a stop to it because it was a matter of time before she became "nice" Mrs Gerund and my bargaining position became totally untenable. Second, by that time, the first week of September was ridiculously close.

'There's a lot to pack, Mum. It'll take a while to decide what you want to take and what you want to get rid of.'

'Phooey.'

Do you know what "phooey" means when used by a geriatric of sound mind and stubborn temperament? It's the equivalent of my saying "I hear what you say" to someone with whom I'm negotiating. No agreement, not even any semblance of recognition that I have a sliver of a point.

My mistake was to think it meant "it'll take no time at all". Mum always believed she could sort things out in whatever time was available. Like nature, Mum abhorred a vacuum (not as much as Dad, whose antipathy to housework knew few bounds) and happily filled every minute with whatever tasks needed doing. While the males in the family flopped in front of the TV in those days when we all watched the same programmes, Mum sat in her straight-backed chair and sewed, darned, ironed, peeled, papier-mâchéd, drew, salted, reupholstered and generally proved multi-tasking was her natural state – we did manage to vote down drilling and cake mixing as too distracting, but those battles were hard won.

What Mum really meant only became clear as we approached the exchange of contracts on the sale which would give us a deadline to work to.

Let us first consider the facts.

1. Mum lived in a five-bedroomed house with three reception rooms, a capacious roof, garage and several sheds.

2. Mum was moving to a two bedroomed, two reception roomed bungalow with a small garage, limited roof space and no shed in sight.

3. As a family we had lived in the house for over thirty-five years.

4. Mum was temperamentally incapable of throwing anything away. They called hers "the make do and mend" generation. More "make do and keep the left overs in case they come in handy some time" generation. The loft was a prime example of "stuffed to bursting", but its situation was repeated throughout the house and outbuildings. When, just after the Textiliste and I bought our first house, Mum extracted from the loft all the books I had ever had between birth and leaving for university, Dad said, as he surveyed the heaps of dusty cartons still left in the attic, 'You know, Barbs, if we ever have to move and really empty this house, it'll spring off its foundations and run for the hills.'

We were on the cusp, therefore, of the Event Horizon, with the home coiled and ready to prove Dad right. It was clearly to be my job to enter and empty that particular black hole which contained every morsel of our family's life for probably one hundred years: every piece of correspondence Dad had had with the gas board, Mum's set designs for every Women's Institute Christmas show from 1975 to 2000, shoes that represented both changing fashions throughout the second half of the twentieth century and the increasing size of our family's feet over the same period and a selection of seventy-eight records that would do justice to a 1950s dance band caller, their presence made all the more remarkable for there never having been any gramophone in the house capable of playing them.

If I had had the time, money and inclination I could have started a museum.

What was it with Dad and the gas board, I hear you wonder? Hmm. Here are two examples.

Sir,

With reference your visit of the 18th inst* I wish to point out that when your engineer assured my wife that the new "natural" gas supply would "blow her away" she didn't expect the gas pressure to be so great it blew the taps off our gas stove...

And this.

Sir,

I would like to thank your engineer for his prompt attendance at our property on the 24th ultimo* when he sought to correct the "gas flow issue". Happily, that problem no longer bedevils us. However, we now appear to have water flowing out of our gas stove. On close inspection that might be due to the feed to the washing machine having been erroneously attached to the stove. We assume this is an error rather than a particularly graphic example of how "clean" the new fuel is....

*For those not old enough to have had these quaint rules of business letter writing beaten into them, inst indicates this month (from the Latin instante mense) and ultimo (from the Latin ultimo mense) means the previous month.

Of course, such historic gems were engaging, but being side-tracked didn't help prepare for the move. In another of those ambiguous conversations I had with my mother, I approached the need to rationalise with calm and consideration...

'Mum, we really need to sort this stuff out now. We only have a couple of weeks.'

'I know, dear. Would you like scones or lemon drizzle?'

'Mum, stop it. This is serious. I... er, did you say lemon?'

'Yes, dear. It is scrummy. I trialled it on Marjorie and she positively swooned. And it slips down especially well with clotted cream....'

'Right, yes. Clotted, you said? Well, ok. Lovely. But in the meantime, the attic?'

She patted my arm. 'Why don't you just move everything into the garage and we can sort it there?'

'But the garage is...'

'I'll make tea.'

'...full.'

'Nowhere is full if you use your imagination, darling.'

She dissembled and distracted and discombobulated and generally proved herself to be a dirty and duplicitous darling. If she'd worked in real estate she would have made a fortune. I had limited time to help. I could do the heavy lifting over weekends, as could the Archaeologist, but we had to leave Mum during the week in charge of the sort-out. We did engage a removal man who provided Mum with boxes to fill with whatever she was taking.

Mr Sodastream also offered a full service, including packing everything. He explained what they did in some depth. Mum listened with just a smear of a smile on her lips. He thought she was giving his offer due consideration. I'd seen that look many times, mostly aimed at one of the men in the family when we had been, well, dullards. There was no way she was going to trust a man to do the packing. Roughly translated the look said:

'Don't be a complete pillock.'

So, I showed Mr Sodastream out, promised we would be ready in good time for his men to load a van and left Mum to begin the process of downsizing.

What a grievous error.

Dad loved politics, especially a debate. He travelled from communist to capitalist and conservative in 40 years. But what he never lost was his distrust of authority, of people telling him what to think. In his judgement, politicians needed to listen more and hector less. This poem is one of the few where his political core can be spied.

The Silent Majority

We are the people of village and town
Of lane and city street.
We are called the 'Silent Majority'
And we know how to vote with our feet.
*

We are the folk who stand in queues
And dutifully wait our turn,
And 'They' think we're just a flock of sheep,
But 'They' have a lot to learn.
*

We prefer to live by the rule of Law
And not to argue or fight.
But 'They'd' be unwise who sought to impose
A doctrine of Might is Right.
*

In the pub, if we talk about politics
The argument seldom gets fraught,
And we don't get too emotional
Unless we're discussing sport.
*

But 'They' shouldn't take us for granted,
For we are a stubborn breed
Who, if hard-pressed will remember
Our forefathers' basic creed.
*

That all are equal within the Law,
Exception is given to none.
That freedom of speech and freedom of thought
Are the rights of everyone.
*

Ignore these truths at your peril,

You subtle political men,
Be your seat of power in County Hall,
Or the shadow of Big Ben.
*

Be you rabble-rousing demagogue,
Or owner of half the shire,
Remember that when the People awake
They will recognise a liar.
*

For we it is who hew the wood
And draw water from the well,
And we will, too, in God's good time
Your transient powers dispel.
*

And when the wells are all run dry,
And all the oak rough-hewn,
We who pays the piper
Will finally call the tune.
*

For England's tale was ever thus
Which he'd be a fool to deride,
And at the final reckoning
The People will decide.

Seventeen

The Mysterious Purpose Of The Glass Bowl

It was two weeks before the designated move when Mum and I began to pack her kitchen.

I mentioned Mum's sign earlier: *No matter wherever I place my guests, they always like my kitchen best.* As a family, we spent most time in the kitchen.

And while there Mum cooked, she prepped, she bottled and she preserved, she peeled and she pummelled. Over the years the combination of her love of cooking and her inability to get rid of anything meant every cupboard and every drawer was chock full.

Add to that two dressers in the garage that were also full of equipment and you had enough stuff to set up a catering college with the left-overs sufficient to back up the Great British Bake Off.

I began well.

Two cracked and chipped casserole dishes were unceremoniously given the heave-ho. A teapot, once a favourite but now with a spout that poured side-saddle, went the same way.

But then I reached the heatproof glass bowls, collected over decades. Often Mum made pies and puddings in these which she then froze. Her glass bowl collection was impressive by anyone's standards.

I pulled them all out and lined them up along the counter in size order. There were four different sizes and thirteen bowls in total.

'Ok. How many?'

Mum glanced my way. 'Thirteen'.

'No, I meant how many are you taking?'

'I know you did.' She did that infuriating smile she saved for these "gotcha" moments. 'And so did I.'

I needed a moment to work back through our conversation to realise she really meant it. 'You can't take all of them.' Ok, yes, I sounded a little petulant. And miffed.

'Why not?'

'There isn't space.'

'How do you know that?' She was now meeting my gaze with a steady stare. It would be "steely" if she hadn't been fighting off a grin.

'Mum, your kitchen is a third larger here and…'

'Haven't you heard of space saving?'

'Of course, Mum, but…'

'And that lovely** kitchen designer said my new kitchen had the latest in space-saving cupboards.'

** *note the "lovely" – if this particular form of endearment was added as an appellation it usually spelt disaster to argue with such a person's opinions – the equivalent of telling Stephen Hawking he couldn't add or that David Attenborough was being unkind to animals.*

'I know, but…'

'Please don't interrupt my flow… the lovely man told me my new kitchen has a greater capacity than the old. He's very clever; he says I can now squeeze in more per cubic metre*** than before.'

*** *this was the clincher; even if her inexorable Ganges of Logic hadn't already swamped me, if someone – anyone – could get Mum talking in cubic metres, nothing I might say would carry any weight whatsoever.*

'I get it. You think all this,' I swept an arm around her kitchen, 'will fit into the new one.'

'No, darling.'

'No? I don't understand.'

She hugged me. 'I know you don't.' She looked up, smiling her goofy smile, chucking my cheek – is there a more annoying motherly gesture ever devised? 'You are as impulsive as your father…'

Pausing here for a moment, the expression *you are as [add characteristic] as your father* has been adopted by the Textiliste in what might be described as a "braking" expression.

Describing something I have said, or worse, have done, or indeed, am in the process of saying or doing thus, renders me instantly immobilised. I adored my dad, but comparisons with, say, his politics, his ranting at the radio, his ideas on best business practice, DIY, house buying, his driving, his… well, you get the idea - does not cut it.

I am different. As in DIFFERENT. I shaved off my moustache, for heaven's sake, in 1998. Didn't that show my intention to be my own man (ok, so I was forty-two, but I don't like to rush)? So, for Mum to make such a comparison was, as she well knew, liable to (a) make me bristle, (b) become defensive, and (c) instantly do the opposite of what I was about to do. Namely argue with her.

'I'll put the kettle on. The thing is, darling, it may not all fit and if so we can decide then what we do with the extras but, unlike your father (and implicitly, me), I prefer not to make assumptions based on a flawed thinking.'

'Which is what?'

'That just because I want to move means I want to get rid of anything.'

'Anything? Haven't we only been discussing glass bowls?'

'I think they are what you lawyers call a test case.'

'You mean you expect to apply the same logic to everything in the kitchen.'

Her smile grew, Cheshire-cat like. She didn't respond, at least not verbally and just held my gaze. It was a caring, teacherly face. One I saw many times as a child when I couldn't grasp a concept: like algebra or ironing a shirt. She knew I would grasp it eventually; I just needed time to absorb what she had said and my subconscious would do the rest.

'You don't mean you plan on taking everything,' my waving arms described windmills of arcs encompassing the house, the garage and beyond, 'with you and then sorting it out?'

She had the grace to giggle. 'That would be logical, captain.'

I didn't give in easily. I dutifully ate my cake (apple and cinnamon) and drank my tea while testing the edges of this theory. But she'd planned it out, even to the extent of agreeing the arrangements with the removal men. All the boxes that contained the absolute essentials (no, I didn't dare ask how she'd identified these) would go to their chosen destinations in the bungalow. Ditto the furniture (Mum had ten sofas and chairs and expected them all to come). The rest would be stored in the garage. And the summerhouse we were having installed. Or, at a pinch, in the sitting room which was the biggest room in the new place.

Gradually, a box at a time would be emptied, its contents reconsidered and, if found essential, or likely to be, it would be kept. If it failed that test it didn't go. Oh no. It was repacked. Once every item had been reconsidered, if there was space left over, some of the non-essentials would be kept (because you never knew, did you?). If, however, there wasn't space then a clear out would be instigated.

Mum was now into her eighties; of course, there were circumstances when she might need thirteen glass mixing and cooking basins. I just couldn't imagine them.

No one I asked could.

When regaled with this conversation, family members sighed and smiled; friends laughed and said things like 'Isn't your mother great?' and 'Doesn't she have spirit?' and 'It's marvellous she knows her own mind.'

Fuckwits, all of them. It was going to be a nightmare. And that was before the intervention of my sister-in-law.

This poem was written from the heart after my father was made redundant a second time.

Why Me?

Joe was made redundant on a Friday afternoon,
His world came tumbling down just after three,
He went back to his office, sat down and shook his head,
And whispered to himself 'Why me?'
*

He tried to recollect just what it was they said,
Some word or phrase, perhaps, would be the key,
He remembered words like 'rationalise' and 'viable' and 'facts'
But they were not the answer to 'Why me?'
*

'It's nothing personal, Joe,' they'd said, 'You've done a damn good
job,'
'It's just a basic economic fact, you see,'
'And if we had our way, we'd leave things as they are.'
And that left Joe still wondering 'Why me?'
*

He'd worked here now for – how long? Why nearly thirty years,
And at least he'd climbed some distance up the tree.
The department he now managed – surely this was a success?
But all that did was emphasise 'Why me?'
*

And driving home that evening his mind was in a whirl
At nearly fifty-five what would he do?
But the thing that most concerned him was what to tell his wife
Who was surely going to ask, 'Why you?'

Eighteen

Enter The Nemesis

The Archaeologist's wife, my sister-in-law is not formidable. She's kind, caring and of a gentle disposition. She's a bit bonkers too but then so are a number of my family and those to whom we are attracted. Personally, I think non-stereotypical behaviours, which after all is what madness mostly is, add to the gaiety of nations – well, they make charades more fun.

Having apprised the Archaeologist of my lost battle on the pre-move downsizing front (he took it with the expected resignation) he informed my SIL. She didn't say much, but the next weekend we all arrived early to continue helping with the packing.

'I'll start on the food then.' SIL headed for the kitchen.

We all knew a fair proportion of Mum's cupboards held every spice, packet, tin and jar imaginable. Most would not be needed in the couple of weeks until the move day. I went upstairs to empty the airing cupboard (I found some lavender drying in the back, hidden by a Matterhorn of towels, which I'm pretty certain was ten years old). It was like packing my gran. The Archaeologist and Mum made for the garage to begin the task of deciding if any of the wood she had saved down the years could be burnt on a planned bonfire – neither of us had much hope, but as it turned out even Mum recognised her days at the lathe were numbered).

Thus, it was a couple of hours before we returned to the kitchen for a tea and cake break (apricot and date, with an exceptional cardamom cream – I keep a diary, that's how I know!)

I suppose I was expecting a number of filled boxes, but there were only a couple. Instead, on one counter-top were a series of tins, jars and packets separated into sections. Mum's frown was one of suspicion.

Stepping back for a moment, I should add that Mum never made a secret of the fact that she had always wanted a daughter and her daughters-in-law were special to her, as the nearest substitutes she had. Unspecified "circumstances" meant Mum and Dad stopped expanding the Le Pard dynasty at me. That said, the lack of a woman on to whom she could pass her many skills left something of a void. I know, that's a bit sexist, but indulge her please; in her sphere of influence women were demonstrably the stronger of the species, so she didn't waste her energies on proving the already self-evident. Said void was, however, filled, to her delight, with her daughters-in-law, both of whom are crafty women (yes, I do mean that in every sense). But there was one trait she understood better than we mere men, we quintessences of dust, and that was that her DILs didn't accept the same BS from her that her sons did.

And therein lay the problem we were now confronting.

'Ok, Barbs.' My SIL absently moved a jar slightly back into line, avoiding eye contact all the time. 'I've set out here,' she indicated a line of maybe twenty containers, 'the items you have to throw away, just so you can decide if you want to replace them. Then there are these which you should dump if you were sensible.' Yes, we all noticed the implication, as my SIL moved down the row. 'And the rest are those which you could keep, but it would be better if they went too. I've packed the rest.'

There was this tone in my SIL's voice that, to me, didn't suggest she was commencing negotiations. More "just sign here".

Mum didn't even approach the items. 'They're all fine.'

My SIL was prepared. She picked up a label-less metal lump that may have been a tin once but now resembled the sort of clinker you might find at the bottom of a steel smelter. 'This had "mangoes" written on it in marker pen. It was pressed against the hot water pipe at the back of the cupboard. I think the contents have been cooking for some time.'

Mum shrugged but didn't fight. 'What's wrong with that one?' She pointed at the tin next to it.

'It has a "use by date" of August 2003. That's three years past.'

'Phooey. They put those on so gullible fools buy new when they don't need to.'

'Barbs. You can hear the contents bubbling inside.'

'We had tins I bought in the war which I used to feed these two boys ten years later and it didn't affect them.'

My SIL looked from me to my brother and her expression suggested she found that statement debatable. However, she merely dropped the can into a black bag she was holding and waited for Mum.

Mum pursed her lips. 'I'll dig it out after you've gone.'

'We'll take it with us.'

By now, Mum was alongside my SIL staring at the three sections of comestibles. She picked up a jar, inspecting the label. 'This hasn't passed its date.'

My SIL looked at it. 'That is because you've had it since before they introduced sell by and use by dates.' She looked at the Archaeologist and me. 'I looked it up on my phone. This brand ceased before then.'

The debate rumbled on for a while, but with each victory for my SIL – she was a midwife so carried a certain authority in the health and safety arena - Mum's shoulders sagged. We men watched, both marvelling and saddened.

Mum must have noticed the less than positive body language of the marginalised. With an edge to her voice, that brooked no argument, she turned on us. 'Well, you two are very quiet. What do you think?'

I looked at him; he looked at me. I knew we were both of the same mind, as we had been since we could both speak. We might be, in aggregate, over one hundred, but some things do not change. He was the one brave enough to articulate the thought.

'Can we go outside and see what happens when we open those mangoes?' He looked at me. 'It might explode!'

After all, scientific research has always taken precedence over all else in our eyes.

Another birthday poem.

To Barbs
October 21st, 1986

On other people's birthdays it isn't really hard
To write lots of jolly verses to put inside their card
The idea is to make 'em smile and I often find that I'm
Already giggling over some atrocious rhyme.
*

But that's for other people, members of the crowd
Bawdy, silly doggerel meant for reading out loud
And though I must admit I love the laughter when it starts
It's all just flippant fun from my mind and not my heart.
*

But writing in your card, my love, on this your special day
Is a very different matter 'cos the things I want to say
Are all pent up inside me and they're sometimes mixed with tears
For I love you very much and I have through all the years.

Nineteen

Sometimes You Can't Take It All With You

Eventually we packed. I dreaded the move day itself for any number of reasons. My children were not speaking to me because I was letting Grandma sell her home which was inextricably linked to all sorts of happy memories of being spoilt rotten.

Taking that away was painful even if I carefully explained the reasoning why the house was too big and the garden too much of a burden. They understood, intellectually, but emotionally they thought I hadn't tried hard enough.

Mum wasn't exactly the life and soul either. She had pretty near exhausted herself getting packed up and fending off not only my SIL but a reinvigorated Archaeologist who had begun to sneak stuff off to the dump.

There had also been some last-minute complications at her new house, involving the video entry system. We'll delve into that later. Suffice it to say that having the engineers around when she was moving gave her grounds for one of her rare grumbles. Said grumbles were always like a sort of personalised cumulonimbus looming over the horizon threatening thunder – often they passed by, but be careful if you caught their full force. As they were humming and haaing over the video, I was charged with reprogramming the doorbell (it came with about forty different settings – it was one of the few things she had left in situ). I spent a futile few hours failing to find the promised tune – something by Louis Armstrong – and always ending up either with the Bee Gees or Max Bygraves. I even failed to turn it off and at one point I had it on permanently – that was the nearest I came to hear her swear at me.

In the end the engineer took five minutes away from his problems and set it in a trice; I think I said thank you, but the beating my ego took just then was probably too much to enable me to stay polite.

In fact, the day itself worked out okay. The removal company were grand. The move was efficiency itself and, ensconced on a chair by the door so no one had to risk using the bell, well-wrapped against a sharp wind and supplied with tea, Mum directed the box carriers to their destinations with aplomb. She also spent some time in the kitchen, helping unpack the essentials while we, of the middle generation, set up her bedroom and the bathroom. By the end of a long day we had her ready and only another one hundred and seventeen boxes still to empty.

In the way of these things I was the man left behind to make sure nothing remained at Silver Crest - the much-loved name of the family home. The removal men knew they could ask me any question about what had been agreed to be left.

When they mentioned the two hundred plus plastic flowerpots that still languished behind the shed I said to leave them. If the buyer complained I'd take them to the dump, but I couldn't foresee that Mum would need them. Just in case I was wrong, I put an assortment of sizes - twenty or so - in my car. How wrong I was to be.

It was a strange feeling, standing in the dining room and looking out of her net curtains onto the front carport and, beyond, the main road. How many Christmases had we eaten there? How many meals with Dad at the table head, distributing home-made wine and philosophy with an equal disregard for the enthusiasm or otherwise of the recipients to receive it?

Mum sat with her back to the window and next to the door, so she could hasten to the kitchen for the next course or extra meat and veg. The Archaeologist sat opposite me, his back to the chimney breast and trapped by Mum and Dad – this made him less likely to be preyed into service by Mum to carry whatever it was she planned to bring through. I'm sure that was coincidental or big brother's privilege.

It had always seemed a crowded room: the large table and eight chairs; the carved oak dresser; the drinks cabinet, known to one and all as the pulpit and now housing a significant collection of home brewed and deadly Calvados, which Dad had acquired during the "twinning years" when the local village, Hordle, found itself linked to Yerville, a small town in Normandy. Now it stretched to a size that seemed unreal. All that remained was the telephone, an old-fashioned version wired to the wall socket and made of British Telecom's choicest puce plastic. It sat, forlornly, on the floor, lost on a sea of oddly well-preserved, if aesthetically dated, carpet.

I hated that phone. There was no privacy and the cord never seemed to stretch far enough away from prying ears. Now it seemed as sad as I was. I knew I should make one last sweep of the house, but I couldn't.

How do you feel when you see someone you've known for ages and with whom you've felt secure stripped bare of all the character that defined them? My children were right; some part of each of those rooms framed a memory of my dad and mum. I can see them now at that table, holding forth or laughing with us. I can smell the roasts, feel the glow of knowing there was a place on the planet where I could go and be loved whatever I'd done or said or thought or felt. Just as I'd shed many layers of skin into that oddly fresh carpet, so I had implanted my memories into that room. Sure, they wouldn't be taken away from me, but the sharpness of the recall that comes from a combination of sight and smell would now be lost.

I locked the front door and got into my car. Mum was excited by her new adventure; had I explained my feelings to her she would have smiled and said, 'You are so like your father. He was a sentimental old pillock too. Now what say you make me a Pimm's and don't you dare drown it.'

This is a piece of prose that Dad wrote for the fortieth anniversary of VE day, in May 1985. In it he reminisces about how he recalled the outbreak of WW2.

September 1939

A slight breeze stirred the topmost twigs of my uncle Edgar's Victoria plum {Dad stayed with his uncle and aunt in Cambridgeshire every summer as a boy – in 1939 he was just about to turn thirteen}. The old tree was laden with fruit, rich and rosy-yellow, hanging like swollen raindrops along a gate bar. Overburdened branches sagged, and wasps, already gorged stupid on sweet juice, sluggishly shouldered their way into soft, ripe flesh.

On my own, in the long grass I gazed upwards, squinting against the flickering sunlight. Leaves rustled, and a plum, half-filled with wasps, thudded quietly into the grass. For a few moments the disturbed occupants stopped eating and murmured crossly.

Now only the sun seemed to move, warming my face as it rose higher above the trees. I daydreamed, in a world all green and golden and fragrant with the perfume of my aunt Mabel's Sweet Williams.

My eyelids drooped.

I heard the kitchen window being opened and my uncle saying, 'Turn on the wireless, Mabel.' There was a peculiar whistling sound. The wireless set was warming up. Atmospherics scratched and crackled, then a tinny voice said '__ no such undertaking has been received and consequently this country is at war with Germany.'

I lay still. Down in the orchard a wood pigeon was cooing drowsily. Near my head there was another squashy thump. It was a marvellous year for plums.

Twenty

Shifting Gear

Mum settled to her new home quickly and, I suppose, I imagined life might become more stable. However, there were the occasional wrinkles. Her new car, for instance. It appeared to work well. It had none of the eccentricities of the old family Rover, no random turning on and off of the headlights, no strange smell that would appear after thirty minutes of driving and then be gone by the hour, but during its appearance you had to wonder how many cats had been incontinent in it. Mum had lost her sense of smell many years before, so it never troubled her, but others could only wince and try and ease the window down a fraction.

So far as I could judge the new car was a success all round. That is until my aunt, Mum's sister-in-law, called. Aunt tended to call when she wanted to chastise me.

'You need to sue them.'

'Hello, Annie. Who?' None of my family are great at announcing who they are and, to be fair, each has a distinctive voice, albeit with a common theme amongst the women of treating all the males as halfwits.

'The garage, of course. Your mother should never have bought French.'

It turned out Mum had broken down and Aunt had rescued her. The car was now back at the garage being repaired. It was nearly eighteen months old. Mum agreed (especially the bit about the French) with Aunt – unusual enough in itself and perhaps a sign I should have noted with more alarm than I did.

The next day I called the garage, having ensured my most pompous "do you know who I am" voice was all unpacked and ready if needed. Mr Gates was the owner; he knew my parents well, as Mum and Dad had taken their various cars to him for many years. My father respected him for his knowledge even if he did sometimes feel he could hear the meter whirling whenever Mr Gates lifted the bonnet as he undertook a preliminary inspection of whatever was ailing it. This is an approximation of how Dad would describe such encounters:

'Oh dear, Mr Le Pard (fizz-click £30), I'd say your carburettor (whirr-ping £42.50) is undergoing a post traumatic (plink-fuzzle

£72.50) aerated seizure of the reverse thrusting (phtang-phtang-strempolop £93.75, plus labour) drongle-faggot.'

If only Dad had been as imaginative when it came to self-help as he was making up car part names.

'Mr Gates? Geoff Le Pard. My mother…'

'Ah yes, your mother. Has she decided on an automatic yet?'

I rather bristled at this. I mean this was a classic diversionary tactic and I, an experienced city lawyer, was not about to be fobbed off. 'Now see here, Mr Gates…'

'It's her deaf aids, you know.'

'What?' The man was clearly feeble-minded.

'I told her before, if she used her deaf aids then she might manage a manual, but if she persists in her love of silence then she needs an automatic.'

Ok, he was good. 'Can we back up a fraction? My mother's car has broken down?'

'Indeed.'

'And it is still under warranty?'

'Yes.'

'And the problem is a part of the car?'

'The clutch is useless, that's true.'

'So, you'll repair the clutch?'

'Of course.' By now I had definitely detected a certain amused tone. I waited. 'Of course,' he went on with a definite timbre to his diction which evoked gold-dusted chocolate truffles being savoured, 'it won't be covered by the warranty. It is caused by your mother's driving style. She rides the clutch like the sugar plum fairy on amphetamines (I don't remember his analogy exactly, but you get the picture). If she put in her deaf aids and could hear the poor thing being shredded she might have avoided this. And, of course, if she had a sense of smell, well, she would have noticed the inevitable stench of massacred metal and plastic.'

I wanted to defend my mother, the family driver, the woman who'd driven cars for Eisenhower or at least some wartime big wigs, but it all had a ring of truth.

'I've no doubt you'll want to discuss this with your mother, Mr Le Pard.' At least this time there was something else in his voice, some shared sympathy. A moment of mutual understanding, like British and German subalterns staring at each other across no-man's-land, sent to do battle but realising they had more in common with each other than those on their own side. 'I'm sorry, Mr Le Pard.'

I retreated, somewhat deflated. I called Mum. 'He suggests an automatic.'

'Humph. He's trying to rip me off. Your father always said he sounded like a taxi meter.'

'He says you don't use your deaf aids while you drive.'

'Why would I use them for driving?'

'To hear.'

'Darling, I like to drive in silence. I find I concentrate better than having the radio on.'

'He says the clutch is completely worn out.'

'Well, I know that. It's because it's French. Did you tell him it's because it's French?'

'No, Mum. He said he'd sort it out.'

'Good. He indicated to me he expected me to pay for it. Trying to take advantage. Still, well done you. Irritating it needed a man for him to see sense but better that than me paying the charlatan. I hope he apologised.'

'Yes, he did say he was sorry.'

I paid. Ok, so I had eighteen months in which to persuade Mum either (a) to get an automatic or (b) to stop driving or we would be funding yet another clutch. Or so I thought.

Her driving was getting worse, not helped by her eyesight. She had, unknown to me for another year or so, cataracts in both eyes which, eventually, she informed me "needed to ripen" before they could be operated on. How much could she see? How dangerous was she? I never probed, just tried to point out the need to be safe.

A new clutch was fitted and the Archaeologist and I were bombarded with suggestions from our wives that we consider telling her it was time to stop driving. We prevaricated. We repeated the "let's try an automatic" plea. It fell on deaf ears (ha!).

Mum went back to her local trips and the issue of the car faded into the background. Mum would tell me if something was wrong and meanwhile I had other things on my plate.

Let me jump ahead here. I have, I think, established I was a coward and failed to grasp the "you shouldn't be driving" nettle. I was sufficiently craven that I used all sorts of subterfuge to ensure she didn't drive if we used her car. We both knew there was a conversation we should have, but I avoided it and she ignored it. Indeed, I think it is fair to say that the car wasn't much of a topic until another call about a clutch sometime in the middle of 2009.

One point to bear in mind. The reason, the sole reason, I knew about the failure of the clutch the first time was not because Mum wanted me to handle the garage; she was more than capable of doing that. It was because my aunt rescued her and therefore I was told of the problem. Aunt may be loyal, but, in that instance, she broke the rules of the Grey Sisterhood which are:

Rule 1: Whatever happens, don't tell the children.

Rule 2: There is no rule 2.

I anticipated, I suppose, when Mum went through clutch number one, that sometime around about eighteen months later, the new clutch would go and I would have to sort it out.

So it wasn't that much of a surprise to be called – by Mum this time – and be told her car (or "ka-ka" as she now called it, because it was French and a "heap of ka-ka") had broken down again. This time she had been rescued by a lovely young couple one evening, on her way back from a birthday for a WI friend. Mum gave them my phone number at the time, as they felt they should call someone. It was only later I found this out and realised that, but for that, I might never have heard of the latest farrago.

It was the concern that I might learn of what had happened from these strangers that prompted the call. Mum called it "keeping me informed"; I called it "managing my expectations". Dad would not have been surprised.

After telling me the about the breakdown and the sweet young couple, the relevant part of our conversation that day went something along these lines. Mum first.

'I'm really disappointed with that French car. Another clutch's gone. It really is rubbish.'

'I suppose it has been about eighteen months since the last one, Mum. The first one went after eighteen months. And you are a little heavy on the pedals…'

Pause. 'I had this one changed three months ago.'

Longer pause from me. 'Three months ago? You never said.'

'I know you're busy, darling. Mr Gates fixed it quickly. He's very efficient.'

'Yes, well. Still, three months is ridiculous; they should last longer. I'll call the garage…'

'No, darling, I'm just sounding off. I can do that.'

'No, Mum. You don't have a lawyer in the family and not allow me to exercise my snotty know-all self. Dad would have said "you don't keep a dog and bark yourself", wouldn't he?'

She didn't fight and let me have my day as Shouty Mr Grumpy. I should have seen that as a sign.

I called the garage, girding my loins for a bit of a fight, but feeling I was firmly on the moral high ground this time.

'Hello, Mr Gates. I'm ringing about my mother's Peugeot. Barbara Le Pard.'

'Ah yes. We spoke before, didn't we? Couldn't get her to buy an automatic, could you? She's a lovely lady, your mum. Stubborn but…'

'Stubborn? She doesn't want an automatic, Mr Gates. She just wants a clutch that lasts longer than three months.'

'That's why she needs to move to an automatic. She's too heavy on the clutch for a manual.'

'Yes, but three months? That is ridiculous. They have to be built to last longer than three months.'

'In normal conditions, yes.'

'Mr Gates, my mother isn't driving up Everest or something.'

There was a pause, a background scuffling that sounded like he was shutting a door before he said, 'Can I explain about clutches, Mr Le Pard?' Odd how formal we had become. 'If you ride the clutch hard it wears out; if you have a car where the clutch has gone once, the next one, under similar conditions, will go more quickly.'

'Yes, but this one went after three months.'

There was a noise like he was rifling through papers. 'Two months and twenty-three days.'

'Really? That's worse. How do you go from eighteen months to two months something?'

'Your mother barely takes her foot off it. When a clutch goes and is replaced then it weakens the surrounds. The next clutch will last a shorter time under the same conditions and so on.'

'But this will be three clutches inside three years and the last one is only two months old…'

'Three?'

Oh dear. The inflection in his voice could have been surprise or delight at what was coming. 'Yes, three clutches.' I was beginning to wonder if he was a half-wit; or maybe I was just hoping he was.

'Your mother told you she has only had three clutches?'

95

Long pause. 'More?'

'Let me check.' By now I could definitely hear the smile in his voice. 'She's had six clutches altogether in addition to the original...'

'Six?!'

'... not forgetting the three gearboxes.'

'Oh...'

He allowed me time for this to sink in. Or maybe to compose myself. I thought he was doing well not to laugh. 'Shall I send you a brochure for our automatic range? Or she could put her deaf aids in and hear for herself what she's doing.'

I told the Archaeologist. We debated telling our wives. We dissembled. In the end, we decided on a better tactic. We lied. I told Mum there was a problem with the Peugeot which meant we had to sell it and the Archaeologist put a deposit down on an automatic. By then she had made up her own mind. The car was getting too difficult anyway and the accumulation of illnesses that would eventually do for her was weighing her down. She never did drive again.

My parents loved France and all things French and they formed a significant and loyal part of the twinning group that ventured regularly to Yerville in Normandy staying with Jackie and Martine. Inevitably Dad was called upon to write a poem to celebrate the tenth year of that twinning.

The Hordle/Yerville Twinning

From an excellent beginning
The Hordle/Yerville Twinning
Has prospered, and now reached the age of ten.
It's agreed by everyone
That it's been a lot of fun,
(With just a few small hiccups now and then!)
*

We've taken them to London,
To the Tower and Hampton Court,
And they've showed us the Palace of Versailles,
And fond memories remain
Of our trip along the Seine,
With the dome of Sacre Coeur against the sky.
*

We have been to Monet's garden,
Seen irises in bloom,
And they have gazed on Salisbury's soaring spire.
They have visited St Paul's
Walked Southampton's city walls,
And on Sundays we have heard the Yerville choir.
*

They have seen our lovely Forest,
We've admired old Honfleur,
And enjoyed the parties in the Salle de Fete,
And on Remembrance Day, each year,
We have shared our silent tears
In memory of those we won't forget.
*

We've had musical exchanges,
Football matches and Scout camps,
We like croissants, they like fish and chips,

There's been picnics by the sea,
A traditional cream tea,
And all, we've shared some most exciting trips.
*

We have seen a lot together
In every kind of weather,
'Cos 'fun', in French and English, means the same.
And however dull the day
It's been laughter all the way,
And getting damp is just part of the game.
*

For example, who'll forget
Feucamps in the wet?
And after lunch it rapidly got wetter
But it was warm and dry
In a cafe quite close by,
And with coffee (and a 'Calva') we felt better!
*

Yerville have an English 'phone box
And a sturdy Forest oak,
In Rue de Hordle both now proudly stand.
While their handsome seat in Hordle
Invites passers-by to dawdle
And study the inscribed milestone, near at hand.
*

Every country has its culture,
Time honoured truths (and lies!),
Likes and dislikes, superstitions, ancient blames,
But friends together always find
They leave prejudices behind,
For, underneath, we're very much the same.
*

And so, ten years have passed,
It's time to raise a glass,
(Or if you're Yervillaise, then lift a 'verre'!)
We've had a lot of fun,
Next millennium – here we come!
Welcome, Bienvenu – both here and there!!

Twenty-One

The Eyes Have It

It wasn't immediately apparent to anyone that my mother's eyesight was deteriorating. She was very good at covering things such as being nearly blind in one eye and close to it in the other. I don't remember her saying she had cataracts, not until she'd been settled in her bungalow for quite a while, but she must have done so at some point, I suppose. About her eyesight, we had this sort of conversation:

'Mum, if you can barely see, how can you drive?'

'It's my eyes that are changing not the roads.'

'Well, given the potholes we have out there I might beg to differ. But that's not the point...'

'Darling, the doctor's is in the same place, so is the supermarket and the WI hall. I know those roads backwards. And I think you are being rather discriminatory.'

'I'm sorry? How do you reach that conclusion?'

'Well, you wouldn't stop a blind man going to the shops, would you? They often memorize the route, don't they?'

'But, Mum, I'd stop a blind person soon enough if they attempted to drive.'

'Exactly. I'm not blind. Obviously if I was I'd stop.'

I tried, really, but all I would be told was she was on the list to have the operation and when they were "ripe" – how I loathed that way of describing them – she would have them done.

Finally, the optician agreed and she was booked in. By this point the glasses she was wearing – varifocals – were enormous, like the windows in a bathysphere. I asked if she wanted me with her, but I was told not. One of her WI friends would see her home.

Fortunately, with so many residents of a vintage hue – South Hampshire is not Costa Geriatrica for nothing – the operations were done at the local surgery.

In advance of the first operation – one eye would be done on the Monday; if all went well, the second eye would follow two weeks later – she arranged for friends and family to pop in. 'Don't come down specially, darling. You're a busy man.'

I did feel a bit guilty, but it was frantic in the legal world back then.

Mum was quietly excited: 'It's very clever. They'll give me a long-distance lens in the first and a mid-distance one in the second. If I need help reading I can get some reading glasses.'

It all sounded grand. I just hoped Mum had heard right. She was convinced that the operation would be a success, just like she was convinced most men were potentially useful if properly trained.

That said, I had found, before this, that when visiting a specialist, my parents didn't always hear what they were told; with Dad's cancer, for instance, they were so stunned that I went to see the oncologists myself to understand what they had said and the treatment options. Mum and Dad couldn't process it for ages.

Anyway, she would have the first operation, have a cup of tea, be taken home and for two days keep the eye-patch on. The only time she was to take it off – it was there to stop her accidentally rubbing the operation area – was, briefly, a couple of times a day to put in drops and at night. Assuming the doctor was happy, the second operation would follow.

The operation went well. So far so good. On the Wednesday, the bandage could come off. I rang for an update. 'Well?'

She sounded low. 'Disappointing if you want the truth. Everything's still distorted.'

'Oh.'

But Mum didn't do low for long. 'The doctor says sometimes it takes a while for the brain to adjust. I just need to be patient.'

We didn't talk for long; I could tell she was upset. She had set her sights (sorry) on better vision. To be able to read again. I was due to visit at the weekend. Maybe things would have improved by then. I went back to the coalface and mined another contract.

Thursday about two pm. My PA appeared at my door. 'It's your mum. She's really anxious to speak to you.'

Honestly my heart fell. Neither parent ever rang at work unless (a) they were abroad and they'd been utterly discombobulated by the time difference or (b) it was an emergency.

'Hi, Mum. What's up?'

'My eye! It's working! I can see everything.'

I was a touch confused. Mum always got up about seven am, as regular as a diet of fresh vegetables and ex-lax. So why not ring me first thing when she took the bandage off? Surely the improvement wasn't so sudden it had just "happened"?

'I'm such a silly.' She almost giggled. Like a schoolgirl. 'I was just watching Grand Designs – that McCloud man is so irritating. I mean, it's not like he does all the hard work himself and...'

'Mum, your eye.'

'Oh yes, sorry. Well, it was foggy. Not here, it's blue sky. It's a bit early for fog anyway, though I expect if I looked at your father's diaries I'll find some time when...'

She did gabble when excited.

'Mum, please...'

'Yes, so I thought I'd better clean my glasses, to help see in the fog,' no, I didn't ask either, 'and when I glanced at the picture the TV was clear. Well, of course at first, I thought there must have been fog in the TV programme and it had cleared or it was just some bad editing, but then I realised it was me. My eyes have suddenly started working.'

I smiled at the picture of Mum and Dad that sat on my desk. Dad would have teased her rotten for not realising her mega-watt glasses were distorting her now perfectly good eye rather than helping. She knew that too, but I was the young apprentice and had to be careful at exercising my teasing rights to the full.

'That's marvellous, Mum. Really. You can throw away the milk bottle bottoms you have for glasses then. I'll see you Friday.'

The rest of the week went well, so I was relaxed as I walked to her front door, two evenings later. I couldn't help smiling. This was good news. Mum always liked to open the door, even though I had a key, and give me an immediate hug. This one would be especially warm. I rang the bell and waited for her lovely fulsome smile.

The door opened to her already retreating back. Not a hint of a hug. 'I need a word with you.'

Not happy. Not happy at all.

She stopped when we reached the kitchen where she stood under the first spotlight. She made me stand right in front of her and turned her face up to me. 'You never told me I had wrinkles.'

'I... er.... um...'

'Why did you let me think my skin was still smooth? I'd have changed my make-up, my powder.'

Her eyes were so bad for so long that she never saw the crepey skin taking over from her once porcelain complexion. I was struggling, utterly out of my depth, so inevitably I kicked for the bottom... 'You're eighty-two, Mum.'

'So?'

'Isn't the odd wrinkle to be expected?'

She turned for the kettle to make tea with an irritated puff of her cheeks. 'Why do you men always think you know how we want to look?'

This poem is from 1945 after Dad started his training to become a member of the Parachute Regiment.

Waiting to Jump

We sat and smoked and waited
So early that summer morn
The sergeant chaffed, but no one laughed
We all felt pretty forlorn.
*

The cigarette smoke thickens
And we remember how to pray
For we've been told, should the weather hold
It's our first drop today.
*

We've waited now for an hour and a half
"Oh God! Let it be soon
Or I'll go nuts – will I have the guts
To jump from the balloon?"
*

"I wonder what they're doing at home
Will they think of me today?
How I miss them all!" Then came the call,
"O.K. fellers, you're on your way!"

Twenty-Two

Santa Claus And The Season Ticket

One curiosity about Mum's bungalow is how its exterior reminded me, in style rather than substance, not so much of the family home which she had recently left, but the first home we lived in, in North Surrey, until I was twelve. Number seven Anne's Walk was a semi-detached house which had been built in the 1920s with little regard for aesthetics. That said, inside the two buildings couldn't have been more different. The bungalow surprised us all, in its sensible layout and cunning use of space; the older semi, frankly, had barely any obvious utility beyond its four walls and a roof. As an example, the semi had fireplaces in every room, but they were so small as to give off little heat while burning unconscionable quantities of fuel. The one in the bedroom which I shared with the Archaeologist was smaller than the rest: a narrow emaciated thing whose shaft was more like one of those pneumatic tubes featured in department stores back in the 1960s that were used to send the invoices and money to the accounts.

And yet that crapulous fireplace was the centre of a moment of boyhood wonder that resonates to this day.

Back in the early 1960s, Dad commuted to work on a steam train; for me, a little boy with small knees and a big imagination, that was so very exciting . And for one particular year end – maybe 1962 - it proved to be more exciting than Christmas. How can I be sure of that? Is such unfounded confidence in a memory merely proof of the truth that it isn't only computers that need regular defragging?

As I recall I was about six. For most of the year, our bedroom fireplace was boarded up with a piece of hardboard, painted white and into which someone had drilled airholes. I well remember the draughts and the occasional, whistling demon that escaped, usually late when I couldn't sleep.

I was then and remain now very credulous. The Archaeologist was born a sceptic. 'So, this here Santa chappie,' he mused a few weeks before that Christmas, 'is able to squeeze down this chimney and through the board, is he?'

Dad, who wanted everything festive to be fun – Mum was too busy cooking to spend time on idle speculation – explained how Santa would manage this. The Archaeologist remained to be convinced and the debate continued until Mum, seeing my growing distress that Santa was about to disappear in a flurry of geometry, stopped them.

'Measure it.'

'Hmm?' The two mooting males regarded her with the reverence she deserved.

'Take the board off and measure it. Then you'll have an idea of how small he needs to be.'

This was beyond exciting for two small boys. While Dad collected enough tools to fabricate a scale model of the Queen Mary from matchsticks we went and positioned ourselves either side of the chimney breast. Dad arrived and with the first screwdriver dislodged the board. The Archaeologist and I peered at the never before exposed (in our lifetimes) grate. Lying on the concrete floor was a rectangle of bright pink cardboard. I'd never seen anything so pink. There were black letters and numbers on it, a sort of code.

'Well, blow me.' Dad picked it up and studied it carefully. 'How did that get here?'

'What is it?' The Archaeologist displayed the fundamental curiosity that has made him both fascinating and a total pain these last fifty plus something years.

'My season ticket. For the train. This one ran out over a year ago.' Dad handed it to the senior subaltern (the Archaeologist) while other ranks (me) hopped from foot to foot trying to see this printed wonder. 'I normally hand them in when I get the new one.'

Mum was consulted, but no one could explain how this pink ticket had found its way to the long shut up fireplace. While I turned this wonder over in my fingers, trying and failing to decipher the codes, Dad and the Archaeologist took a series of measurements and debated the volumetric challenges of a supersized fantasy figure squeezing down a small bedroom chimney.

I tried to imagine the way, much like the arrival of Mary Poppins, in which the card had been blown on the north wind and ended up waiting to be found. There had to be a message in its appearance but what?

Mum understood the excitement this mystery generated. While I don't remember details, I do remember how she postulated what these curious figures might mean – a code, or some secret message. She let her mind wander onto the card's journey: how did it get there? And why? We boys both loved this exercise in imagination.

I wonder what happened to that card; probably the Archaeologist purloined it: he's collected most things all his life – his house is crammed with stuff. Me, I just needed the idea of the card, lying there, waiting, maybe expecting, to be discovered – it was my ticket to a world inside my head, a world of stories to be unfurled and retold.

As for the chimney, well since Santa squeezed down and left us stockings full of chocolate money, satsumas, Betta Bilda blocks (upmarket Lego) and plastic animals for the farm that formed an adjunct to our train set, it was clearly big enough, even if Santa needed a couple of pints at the rugby club in order to manage the contortions.

We also knew by this time not to disturb Santa and Mrs Santa until after seven am while we played with our gifts, if we wanted Christmas Day to start on a positive note. The Archaeologist probably mused on some anatomical faux pas in the design of the okapi while I thought about the journey I might undertake, up that chimney, with the freedom of the pink ticket.

Dad spent three years in Palestine from 1945 to 1948, prior to Partition. He wrote a number of poems to Mum about his thoughts and fears.

Thoughts of Home

I compared the lush brilliance of an orange grove
With the glow of an orchard in Kent
And although I was two thousand miles away
I knew what England meant.
It meant the call of the peewit in winter
Over a darkened ploughland rise
And the song of a lark in springtime
As it climbs into sunlit skies.
An old mill on a river bank
Sheep meadows of fresh grass
They are the thoughts of England
God grant they shall not pass.

Twenty-Three

Other People's Funerals

It is increasingly the fashion that when people die after having had a "good innings" their funerals are structured to celebrate a life as much as to mourn their departing. We had attempted that with Dad with reasonable success. Some though hate the whole idea and for those who are becoming aware of their own increasing mortality, funerals can be unpleasant reminders and not so welcome.

With Mum nothing could have been further from the truth. Obviously, she didn't want her friends to die, but if they did, well, these were opportunities not to be wasted. She had a quixotic relationship with funerals.

First there was the sharing of the news, and the excuse to reprise both the life now over, as well as the mode of death. This need for detail was neither salacious nor gratuitous. Partly it stored up a comparative knowledge that might aid others – "oh yes, Dawn had Prescott's Biblious Grommet Syndrome, but she lasted ten years after the tuna poultices were applied"; partly it allowed for a deepening of the sympathy – "poor Meryl had Crowther's Redundancy Complications, and could never manage cribbage after the third operation".

Then there might be a little light speculation on who might go next. "Dennis is peaky". "Harold has given up Rioja" "Beryl is on the dabs again".

And the type of send-off was an important focus of the debate. "She said quiet, though she liked a do if someone else was paying". "It'll be canapés and warm white. Never did grasp catering did Phyllis".

Of course, there was some mileage to be gained in identifying those who wouldn't be invited. "Dolores is going to her daughter's that day". "Really? No invite?" "Not after the crochet imbroglio".

The songs. "She'll have hymns, the heathen". "Apparently, he wanted Kylie, but Martine put her foot down after that video embarrassment".

So, when Joan, a family friend of some sixty years, died after a short bout of pneumonia, we had to go. Dad went to school with Joan's husband Fred, and they had married a couple of years before Mum and Dad. Sadly, Fred now had dementia, but their sons were organising things and were keen if Mum could make it. 'Not many of their generation left,' was the way their eldest son, a doctor, put it to me. 'Dad mentions your mum. A lot.'

You wondered why he should remember her specifically. But Mum was keen, so I took a day off work and planned to drive her the round trip of one hundred and fifty miles to and from Surrey for the service and wake and then home.

We had a bit of a to do in the car. Mainly because we used hers – "It needs a run" – and I said I'd drive. 'I'm still capable of driving, you know.' Hmm, we left that one hanging.

Then there was the radio. 'It doesn't work properly. I can't turn up the volume.'

'You're not using the right knob, Mum.'

'Well that's a bloody silly place to put it.'

We settled eventually and talked about Fred and Joan and boating holidays in the early 1950s before children. Of Fred and Dad, lean young men, just out of the Forces, showing off by jumping in the Thames and posing for the camera. Of parties. Not exactly sober affairs. Of Fred's old Ford that took them everywhere but hated the many Surrey hills. Apropos of this, Mum said, 'Poor man had one shot off.'

It is difficult to know where to come at a statement like that. I was pretty sure she didn't mean Fred so decided on the who question hoping that the what would be answered too.

The reply came swiftly. 'George Bale. Big bear of a man. Odd nostrils.'

Were they the "what"? Did he lose a nostril? Having one would be "odd" in several ways.

Mum stared out of her passenger window at the recently cut hay being bundled into those huge ball things that pass for haystacks these days. It was a lovely late summer day. 'Fred drove the boys to away games (of rugby). He always tried to avoid taking George because of his size. Said it weighed down the car.'

'Did he have the handlebar moustache? Rode a Triumph motorbike?'

'Wrong George. That was Stuart. Charming man though he did pat a little too much for my liking. Drank Vermouth, too.' This last was said in a way I think meant she suspected his orientation, though that contradicted the tendency to pat women. Mum wasn't someone you patted twice, methinks.

She carried on, warming to her anecdote. 'They had to take George because he'd injured himself. They were off to the hospital which meant going up Church Hill (this is one of the steepest hills in North Surrey) and the car was struggling. When finally, they crested the top and breathed a collective sigh of relief, Fred looked back at George and said, "Just as well you've only got one, George, or we'd not have made it".'

I waited. I know my mother. She was deliberately eking this out, waiting for me to ask the what question. She could out-wait St Peter, that woman. I asked.

'His testicle. Hit by a sniper near Mannheim in 1945. George always said it was as well it was his left one because he was so right handed.'

The funeral was freezing, but we warmed up at the do after. Mum held court, telling nephews and nieces and younger generations about the Fred and Joan she remembered. George's long-ago sniped testicle loomed large as it were. She loved to shock, did Mum. Meanwhile Fred circled the food table greeting Mum with the best smile of the day and a hug of real affection. Mum played along each time, like they hadn't met in ages.

On the way back, Mum was quiet, contemplative. Finally, she said, 'Dementia is a dreadful thing, isn't it? Losing someone you're close to without really being able to grieve and move on. But oddly the new Fred is lovely. Charming. He'd become something of a curmudgeon latterly. This one is much more like the old Fred, the one we holidayed with. I hope his children can appreciate that at least.'

Let us return to the birthday series of poems.

To Barbara – October 21st, 1987

On your special day, my love, the world is touched with brightness,
As the slow October sun, warm and drowsy as a child,
Floods the garden with rich golden light.
Along the tangled ancient hedge, bees quest and murmur in the ivy flowers,
And butterflies, with quivering wings, grow tipsy on the juice of tumbled apples,
Soft-decaying in the dappled orchard grass.
Late roses, petalled pink and red, beckon from the secret corners which are your delight,
While clematis, unscathed as yet by chilly nights, still clambers skywards,
Gleaming star-like through the shady shrubs.
So, nature smiles Her thanks to you today, remembering your gentleness, and loving care,
And I, who love you very much, smile too, but cannot speak,
Lest foolish tears betray a trembling heart.

Twenty-Four

Self Sufficiency (1) – The Kitchen And The Garden

Mum never lost the urge to save. Not money, per se, but simply to get the most out of whatever she had. In fact, it would be truer to say that she had an overwhelming urge to extend everything as far as it would go. She would make everything she could, from scraps and old bits of what, to most people, might be rubbish. Let us start with her kitchen and a few examples.

Sometime in the late 1960s we acquired a ginger beer plant. All I recall of Mum's experiment now is (a) how fiery her brew was (b) how it never stopped and eventually Dad had to beg her to throw it out because he just couldn't drink any more, and (c) the countless times the corks blew off or the bottles exploded covering her pantry in a sticky film.

This urge to grow something that paid for itself took hold. She did much the same with yoghurt only I don't think she really mastered it because, rather than providing us with good bacteria, as all the adverts promised, my recollection is of this white napalm she offered us for dessert. I could be mythologizing this, and the truth could be that her product was just sour and not to a child's taste. At that time the only yoghurts I had experienced were the French "Ski" brand which were strawberry flavoured and sweet. Mum's answer to any complaint was to add sugar to hers and mash up some fruit and say it was just as good because the ingredients were the same. If only.

Into this mix, I must add Mum's experiments with yeast. Mum didn't ask for much by way of birthday or Christmas presents – it was always about others – save there were two things she wanted and asked to be put on a list. One was a Black and Decker Workmate – a sort of all-purpose workbench – and the other was a Kenwood food processor. This came with a dough hook attachment which it took Mum a while to master. When she did we had a series of Chelsea buns, Bath buns, and a variety of breads and rolls. They were all fabulous though, as with the ginger beer, Dad did plead that she stop making them as he was getting fat. The Archaeologist and I would have had her continue ad infinitum, but she listened to Dad, much to our chagrin.

For her experiments in baking, she grew her own yeast. I can recall the smell – not unpleasant but very rich and sort of beery – and

112

some occasions when she allowed something to prove too long and it swamped wherever she had put it - on one occasion it ended up behind a radiator. She was proud of her baking too, making things for the various WI shows and winning prizes – though out-doing some of her peers probably counted for more than the prize itself.

All these experiments were mere precursors to my parents developing their fruit and vegetable growing and the preserving of the produce that the garden increasingly provided.

By the end of the 1970s the garden was producing so much that my parents invested in a second freezer to store it. Dad's husbandry improved, the quality of the soil increased and we were going to be overwhelmed with vegetable fecundity; had the grow'n'store approach continued, my parents would have been faced with a dilemma: either throw some away or become vegans. Neither was at all likely.

The solution, oddly, was at hand in the shape of my tiny, but formidable, maternal grandmother.

Another birthday poem.

Our Garden

October 21st, 1991

There's a little piece of England that we've made yours and mine
Where we spend happy hours, summer, winter, rain or shine,
In the garden we've created near the Forest and the sea,
Neither too large and not too small – just right for you and me.
*

There are annuals and perennials, plants for sun and partial shade,
And some which seem to glow when daylight starts to fade.
There's a birdbath and gazebo, hanging baskets and sundial.
(And a funny man up in a tree who makes the children smile).
*

On either side the ancient hedge, of holly, hawthorn, yew,
Is columbined and ivy-bound to shelter mouse and shrew,
Summer-smothered pink and white with fragrant, rampant rose,
Then bird-haunted in the autumn when scarlet berries glow.
*

Wisteria and clematis stretch fingers to the sky,
And tiny alpines thrive where the soil is hot and dry.
In moist and mossy corners ferns and hostas, dimly seen,
Stand heavy-leaved and statuesque in every shade of green.
*

There's a special place for herbs – sweet marjoram and rue,
Lavender and lovage, dill and feverfew,
Chives and coriander, parsley, mint and sage,
Thyme and balm and borage – names from a bygone age.
*

Away beyond the apple trees and hedges of sweet peas,
Past broad herbaceous borders bright with butterflies and bees,
We grow our favourite vegetables and children love the fun
Of harvesting the produce from spring showers and Summer sun.
*

And so, the seasons come and go, and nothing stays the same,
And failures and successes are just part of the game,
But no matter what the weather – for us it's always fine,

114

In that little piece of England that we've made yours and mine.

Twenty-Five

Self Sufficiency (2) – The Garden Shop

Simply growing veg and fruit would have sufficed for most people but not my mother and, after she moved in, her partner in crime, my gran, Mum's mother.

Gran was a fiercely independent woman who, aged eighty, found coping with her enormous Georgian house on the North Kent coast too much and moved in with my parents. A few months later, and so as not to be outdone, my father's mother, my nana, moved in too. This ménage à quatre continued for some five years until Nana died in the late 1980s. But while it continued Gran tried to differentiate herself by being "helpful".

This often led to conflict, but not much daunted her. One day, Mum and Dad went out and left Gran in the garden peeling runner beans. They would be salted and stored later. A man appeared round the side of the house – no locked gates then.

'I was walking down the lane,' he began – our house adjoined a quiet lane though there was no pavement so not many pedestrians – 'and I couldn't help noticing your magnificent sweet peas. I wondered what the variety was?'

If Gran suspected he was a conman she didn't show it because she offered to find out – Dad kept the seed packet on a stick at the end of any row of seeds he planted, and Gran knew it would probably still be there even if covered by the now huge sweet peas. Dad might have focused on veg, but he loved sweet peas and grew fabulously scented monsters.

The man was suitably impressed and, chatting to Gran, asked to buy a bunch – it seemed he knew with sweet peas the more you cut the more you get.

If there was one thing Gran liked better than nearly anything else, it was making a sale – retailing was in her blood. She persuaded the man to buy a huge bunch and no doubt priced it very competitively.

When Mum and Dad returned, both were delighted until Gran suggested putting a notice by the gate, offering them for sale on a regular basis. Now Dad was horrified and had numerous excuses: even though the lane at the side was quiet we actually lived on a fast busy road so no

116

one would see the sign; no one else would want them anyway; who would sell them; we'd be the victim of theft. And on and on.

Gran, knowing her, didn't argue. She let him think he'd won. Then when he next went out for the day, she made a sign, pulled her deckchair to the front gate and waited.

Once again Dad returned, unaware of what had happened. He found his sweet pea rows devoid of blooms and, indeed, a fair few runner beans picked too. Gran, meanwhile, had a wooden box full of change. Enough to pay for the seeds for all the sweet peas, the beans and a fair bit beside.

Dad might have had a large ego, but it was easily deflated by the sight of so much cash; he was won over, but the battles didn't end there.

Often Gran would happily sell that evening's dinner if not restrained. It was an addiction. She had Mum drive her round to see what other places were charging and made sure we just undercut them. Once we had the local grocer turn up, having heard about some success of Dad's and wondering if Dad grew enough to supply them. No, was Dad's probably correct answer, to Gran's disappointment.

Over time the produce paid for two greenhouses – something Dad had always wanted – and all his seed and lots of tools. People came from miles around. His leek plants became something of his speciality. He knew his were better than anyone else's, especially the garden centres. He had a technique which he wouldn't share with anyone which led to the most awesome prize-winning beauties.

Maybe, had Gran been about during the yoghurt and ginger beer phases, we would have gone in a different direction as a family, but the pleasure all three of them got from the growing and selling eased any friction there might have been. It didn't stop the arguments, mind you…

Mum had a wonderful relationship with her own mother who, in turn, thought her daughter infinite in her wisdom and poise. Not so much Dad who she thought lucky to have met Mum, let alone marry her. But when Dad accepted that Gran should live with them and actually made it quite fun, she mellowed and their relationship, in Gran's last years, was sparky, never dull, often acerbic and full of humour. We had the most splendid ninetieth birthday party for Gran with as many relatives present as we could muster. Inevitably Dad wrote a poem.

To Gran - Ninety Years On (October 7 1986)

On October 7 1896 the Wright Brothers hadn't yet flown
Women were not allowed to vote, Victoria was still on the throne,
Oil was something you put in lamps, the railways ran on coal,
Titanic was just an engineer's dream, Scott hadn't raced for the Pole.
*

The map of the world was still half red, men always stood for the Queen,
And a blacksmith's forge, not a garage, looked out on the village green:
Horses were used throughout the land by baronet, bishop and brewer,
And though no-one choked on exhaust fumes, city streets were choked with manure.
*

Two World Wars were horrors undreamed – except by HG Wells
And on Sunday mornings the only noise in the land was the ring of bells.
Space travel and nuclear power were a million miles away
But a letter cost only a red penny stamp and delivery took just one day.
*

No-one had watched television, or flown, in six hours, the Atlantic,
The countryside lived by the seasons – and the pace was scarcely frantic.
Twopence you needed for ten cigarettes, or a gin, or a pint of beer,
And in the pub you could talk to men who had fought in the cold Crimea.
*

That's how it was ninety years ago, in an England long since gone,

So it's good to know, in this transitory world, that one thing is still
going strong
I refer to Grace Lillian Francis who all through the years, bad and
good,
Kept her powder dry and her head held high as an Englishwoman
should.

*

But this is no time to be serious, too deep or too profound
This is your special day, Gran, with your family all around.
We wish you a Happy Ninetieth Birthday – and bright tomorrows, too,
Gran, with all Our love and respect, we raise our glasses to you.

Twenty-Six

Self Sufficiency (3) – Livestock

Having mastered growing produce and selling it there was, of course, a next stage. The Good Life was being popularised on the TV and Tom and Barbara (how prescient of the script writers to use Mum's name) expanded beyond their vegetables and fruit and included livestock. My parents wondered about a goat. They thought about bees – Dad went on a course that took weeks only to be told our garden wasn't suitable due to the proximity of a riding stables.

In the end they alighted on a rabbit breeding programme.

This was a surprise to the Archaeologist and me; in the late 1960s we had found a rabbit wandering around the woods near us in Caterham where we then lived. After we caught it, Dad built a cage and the fluff ball stayed with us, generally benignly until the day he decided he was fed up being vegan and bit Dad. He swore then – and boy, did he swear – that never again would we have a rabbit.

Which was true because they got a pair.

I don't remember being party to this decision, but I do remember Mum telling both of us that we mustn't name them: 'They're not pets, they will be killed and eaten.' That was ok with us – we both liked rabbit pie.

'Will Dad do the killing?' I'm really not sure why we asked; we both knew the answer.

'No, I will,' this from Mum. Dad was a man's man who could be as squeamish as a Victorian heroine. Oddly this hardened killer trait seems to have carried through the mitochondria and ended with the Vet, dainty blonde and all that, but similarly unsentimental when it comes to meat production – she was the one volunteer to kill and skin a rabbit on an army camp she attended aged circa fifteen, while all the boys turned away. Now she's keen to save them. Go figure.

Anyway, we were now the owners of our own meat source and all the peelings and shed lettuce leaves and what-have-yous were given to Rabbit A and Rabbit B, pending their eventual demise.

And all would have been well but for a film and two cousins.

My two delightful cousins lived a few miles away in the pub their parents ran and would visit from time to time. No one thought to mention the rabbits, and certainly not their fate, when these two bounced into our garden, saw the pen and squealed.

'What are their names?'

'They don't have any. You see...'

Cuz 1: 'This one's Hyzenthlay.'

Cuz 2: 'This one's Fiver.'

Watership Down. A crapulous carbuncle of cinematography. Who'd have thought they would have just seen this?

By the time my parents emerged it was too late to explain. Mum was in a bind. This wasn't the idea at all.

Over the next few weeks the cousins appeared and made a beeline for the bunnies. Mum explained to their parents who told her not to worry. When the time came she should just tell a little white lie – about how they'd gone to a new home. Mum wasn't happy, but it would have to do.

And it would have been fine. But for the Archaeologist. The dread day dawned and the two lapins de dejeuner were re-categorised, and the pen removed.

The cousins arrived and headed for the garden. They looked around for their friends. 'Where are the rabbits?'

Mum swallowed and prepared to explain about the re-homing, but the Archaeologist, undoubtedly having a George Washington moment, interjected. 'They're in the freezer.'

Mum and Dad never kept livestock after that.

And my cousins? I think the counselling is going well...

Dad became well-known, locally, for his poetry and was often called upon, not only to recite, but also to pen something for a friend's birthday or wedding anniversary. He hated being what he described as "a poor man's laureate", writing poetry to order. There are many that were written and few he was proud of. This, however, which he wrote for my uncle and then adapted for me on my forty-fifth, he did quite like.

Maturity

When you're young, in the morning, you've no time for yawning,
You're up, and about, and away,
And though you were tight the previous night
You don't show a sign come the day.

You sing in the tub, have a brisk, healthy rub
With one of those huge hairy towels,
But what you don't do is waste time in the loo
'Cos, of course, you've no problem with bowels!

You dress in a trice, you don't have to think twice,
All your clothes fit and that makes it simple,
And your solitary care, while combing your hair
Is you notice you've still got that pimple!

Hurry up! You'll be late! Ah, that breakfast smells great!
And there's sausage and eggs, too – how nice!
The coffee is made and there's thick marmalade,
Yes, please, I'll have just one more slice!

You eat in a hurry, you don't have to worry
With flab and the weight-watching game,
You're unlikely to bulge even though you indulge,
And tomorrow you'll look just the same!

But we with more years shed sad bitter tears,
Now our prodigal youth has long passed,
Some are happy, they say, to be old, bald and grey,
Not me! I just hoped it would last!

But it wasn't to be, and slim handsome me
(Oh, I was a conceited young cub!)
Is beyond recognition, a poor apparition,
So I think I'll stroll down the pub!

Twenty-Seven

Self-Sufficiency (4) – The House Of Barbara

Mum never stopped sewing; her TV viewing was fractured by the constant dip of her head to check on whatever it was she was working on in the evening, as she sat in her straight-backed chair and multi-tasked. Right to the end of her life you took a risk, resting your weight on the arm of her chair because, more often than not, you would be perforated by an injudiciously implanted needle. Darning, shortening, lengthening, patching, her evenings after dinner kept us clothed without unnecessary expense. But as I arrived at adolescence, the make do and mend, fix it up, style of dress no longer quite cut it.

We grew up in what my parents described as a rural idyll but to the teenage me was the arse end of nowhere; I desperately wanted the kind of life 1970s TV hinted at via some of the more avant-garde programmes, such as Nationwide and Blue Peter. Trips to fun fairs, visits to shopping precincts with cinemas, ice skating and above all the ability to hang out without having to rely on my parents delivering me somewhere in the family car, accompanied as it surely was with a moan. Couldn't I cycle? Did you meet my bike, an early prototype for the bone-shaker of Victorian years?

Hanging out (not that we called it that) with my friends required two things, it seemed to my nascent and barely-there teenage brain: other teenagers and something to sit on. It didn't need New Forest ponies and boggy heathland.

My mother was not an insensitive soul. While she might have abhorred hanging out per se, she understood the psyche that wanted to experience it. But we lived miles from anywhere, a gallon of petrol cost the same as the national debt of sub-Saharan Africa or at least that's how Dad justified not giving me a lift anywhere and, anyway, the sheer awfulness of being taken by my parents and "seen" would have undermined any hanging out credits that might accrue.

Then Mike, my best friend, turned seventeen. He passed his driving test within hours (or so it seemed) of his birthday and since his dad had more cars than the average garage forecourt, we were set.

Except I wasn't. The lack of any hangingoutness experience meant I'd failed to develop a sartorial instinct and my dress sense was more Sesame than Street. Jeans had passed me by, flares were things

124

they shot in the air when boats got into distress and cheesecloth was used to, erm, make cheese, not shirts.

Neither of my parents had any spare readies and when they did the fact they called the pound note a "small green drinking token" told you all you need to know about their spending priorities. It wasn't on clothes.

So, it was with a degree of reluctance but a certain inevitability that I turned to Mum again, this time for her dressmaking skills.

She was game, worryingly so. She took me to the haberdashery department of some enormous store where she delved into their pattern department. 'What style do you want?'

How the hell was I to answer that?

'Denim?'

'That's a material not a style.'

'Jeans and a, erm, jacket.'

Mum had never sowed denim before.

She bought some brushed blue – 'a popular choice madam,' said the pert and prissy salesman, not exactly filling me with any confidence that we had made the right choice – and promptly destroyed five needles on her ancient Singer sewing machine as it fought to penetrate the cloth to make the seams.

It was with reluctance that she gave up and offered me a needlecord alternative.

Again, I chose and a patchwork of red and blue appeared. It was actually admired at the Hawkwind concert I went to, well almost.

You see, to save time she elasticated the waist.

Someone noticed, someone who understood the faux pas that this was.

Laughter. Humiliation. Mortification. But you know what? Those trousers were the most comfortable I'd ever had because they were tailored to my rather bizarrely shaped thighs.

The needlecord was hardly robust, and the trousers soon tore, but Mum was on a roll.

She made me some flares in a check design, a tartan set with straight legs and pink denim jeans (by then Mum had invested some of the garden money into a new sewing machine).

They were unique, ghastly and very me. And all were, to a greater or lesser extent, elasticated.

At the time I'd have given several years of my allotted term and two vital organs for Wranglers or Levis.

Now I'm glad Mum held out and ensured I was unique.

Afterwards, indeed to this present day, I make clothing choices that cause laughter but, because of Mum, I really don't care.

Dad was very proud to call himself a Man of the New Forest and in the thirty-five years he lived there he walked most of it, several times over. He absorbed the lore and the legends and penned several poems based around stories he heard in pubs or read about in ancient dusty tomes. This is one such.

The Setley Plain Gibbet

(an epic New Forest poem – about 200 years ago, the two-body gibbet which had dominated the New Forest skyline between Sway and Brockenhurst for so many years, was at last demolished. This must have pleased the local people, but superstition was very real in those far-off days and for long afterwards strange stories circulated through the remote countryside.)

When I was a young man and not long from school,
Like all braggart youth I was brazen and brave,
And I laughed him to scorn and called him a fool
Who whispered of those who return from the grave.
*

'If they are dead, they are dead – so much mouldering clay,'
'And if you see ghosts you are drunk – or insane!'
And the wager seemed nought in the bright light of day
To spend that night, alone, by the knoll on the Plain.
*

By the time evening came and winter sun set
In a fierce blood-red glow over Wilverly Hill
Every soul in the village had heard of the bet
And my arrogant heart had felt the first chill.
*

For I knew the story like all of us there
Of the Setley Plain Gibbet, which centuries gone,
Had stood high and grim in the very place where
I'd boasted I'd spend the whole night alone.
*

A hillock of bare earth is all that remains
Standing just a few yards from the well-trodden way
Which, crossing the miles of gorse-covered plain
Brings the traveller at last to the village of Sway.

*

Even in spring when the moorland glows gold,
And the warm, scented furze calls the foraging bees,
The ground at this place stays mortally cold,
And no skylark nests here, no pony takes ease.

*

No sun-loving lizard, no close-crouching hare,
No adder loose-coiled seeks this chilly mound,
No beast of the Forest, no bird of the air,
No grass, gorse or heather is here to be found.

*

And a tale was told by the old men of Sway
Of a foolhardy traveller who would not take heed,
Who had to reach Lyndhurst by early next day
And who said his two pistols were all that he'd need.

*

They said he was found with his hair turned quite white,
Eyes fixed and staring and mouth opened wide,
Silently screaming at some ghastly sight
And no mark on his body to show how he died.

*

Just tales? Superstitions of foolish old men?
But my heart filled with terror that pride would not show,
And I drank and waited the dread moment when
Someone would say 'It's time now to go.'

*

Too soon came the call, and into the night,
Drunken and singing we lurched through the snow,
All close round the lantern whose pale, yellow light
In the menacing darkness cast scarcely a glow.

*

And I sang the loudest of all of us there,
And shouted with laughter at each foolish jest,
Then threw out the challenge that I didn't care
If the Devil himself came – he'd soon give me best!

*

And then we were there and the merriment died
As, suddenly sober, we stood in the snow,
But still I flaunted my swaggering pride
And in confident tones urged the others to go.

*

The sound of their voices died quickly away
The gleam of the lantern was soon lost to sight,
As they hurried thankfully back home to Sway
To bolt cottage doors and shut out the night.

*

The air, when the snow stopped, was bitterly cold,
The darkness intense, the stillness profound,
The whole world was silent as, no longer bold,
I fearfully stood by the old gibbet mound.

*

Trembling, I looked to the left and the right,
While the terrible cold froze me through to the bone,
And I knew in my mind though no soul was in sight
That, beyond any doubt, I was not there alone.

*

How can I describe the unreasoning fear,
The primitive terror no thought can prevent,
That came from the knowledge that someone was near,
And directing at me its evil intent?

*

Filled with blind panic I turned and I fled,
Stumbling and sobbing and cursing the night,
Until just as my strength was beginning to ebb
Far ahead I discerned a faint glimmer of light.

*

Faltering now and filled with despair
Like a desperate fox hunted over the moor,
Heart beating madly, and gasping for air
I staggered at last to the furze-cutter's door.

*

Exhausted, defeated, I fell to my knees,
A pitiful, tremulous, terrified wreck,
And then, with infinite horror, I felt
Long bony fingers encircling my neck.

*

I remember no more – I fainted away
With that terrible pressure unbearably tight
And they say that I lay there, half dead, half alive,
Till the furze-cutter came in the grey morning light.

I'm told that for weeks I hovered near death,
Mumbling and muttering and never quite sane,
But then came the spring, and with it my health,
And I became part of the village again.
*

But the memory remains, though so many years gone,
And I sometimes awake in the depths of the night
And though it be summer I'm chilled to the bone,
As the terror returns and reason takes flight.
*

And all that took place when I was a lad,
In that dim, distant past, now so far and remote,
But you don't believe me? Then what is this scar?
This ring of dead skin, like a noose round my throat?
*

And who among you, on this cold winter night,
When the fog is so thick and the village snowbound
Will go out from his house, leave the warmth and the light,
And keep vigil – alone – by the old gibbet mound?

Twenty-Eight

Self Sufficiency (5) – The Aftermath, Or Jumbled Thinking

For Mum to be able to create as much as she did, she needed both a supply of materials as well as somewhere to dispose of what she didn't need. Today the rise and rise of the charity shop – the thrift shop across the pond – provides both an outlet and a source, but back when I was young these beasties didn't exist. In their place we had the traditional jumble sale.

Mum loved jumble sales, especially the ones that she helped run: the glory of going round collecting; the sorting (and surreptitiously secreting the stuff she wanted – she paid for it, of course); and the fun of making money. She couldn't have had a better pastime.

My first encounter with this passion was via Dad's love for sport. Dad enjoyed playing rugby; he was a short-fused, somewhat hysterical hooker for his school's old boys' team, the Old Caterhamians.

The Old Cats played their games on a series of boggy fields at the top of Church Hill behind St Mary's Church. The site was windswept and unappealing unless you actually wanted to play. Once in a while, as small children, Mum would drag the Archaeologist and me along to watch him and have an orange juice after, while Dad tried and failed to maintain the balance between being one of the lads and a committed family man – usually by the expedient of, from memory, resorting to a judicious "I just need to have a word with so-and-so, Barbs" before slipping away and leaving Mum to deal with two bored boys.

I think, were these the only memories I had of the rugger club, as it was called – "rugby" as a descriptive term wasn't used by my parents back then – I don't think they would feature on the "fond" spectrum. But once a year the rugger club held a jumble sale to raise funds. Their needs hadn't historically been great – usually new posts, a set of shirts – but for a time these sales were crucial because of plans to build a new clubhouse and changing rooms; this meant cash, lots of it, was needed.

So, the jumble sale took on a new importance. And Mum, being Mum, led the way with vigour. Some time after Dad passed his driving test in 1962/3, we acquired a car – a Hillman Husky - that was like a van with a hinged door at the back. Primarily this was to cart the dog around, but in the run up to the jumble sale it came into its own.

First up there were flyers; I assume these were printed rather than hand-written, but that would only have been the case if someone worked in a printing shop and got them done for nothing. Otherwise, I'm pretty sure Mum would have written them.

The great thing about the flyers was that we two boys were the deliverymen. Mum would park the car and we would be dispatched to leaflet either side of the road; oh, the joy of running up someone's drive – legally mind you – to push the leaflet through the letterbox.

I learnt several things about letterboxes, namely:

- The low-level ones were always awkward.
- If there was a dog that sounded like it ate boys, the letterbox was both at an inconsiderate height and too wide for comfort.
- Several letterboxes were so sprung-loaded that you could easily take off a finger.

Collecting for jumble sales, like so many things in my young life, seemed to involve lessons in patience. Having posted the flyers, we left them for a week and then returned. This was always after school and before tea. We would do several roads a day, spread over several days. How trusting was my mother? Once again, we boys were dispatched, this time to knock on a door and ask if they had anything for the jumble sale that we had advertised a few days before. I guess we struck lucky two out of five times. Sometimes my mother was needed to carry stuff; sometimes we needed to note the house number so a large rugger playing type could come by; sometimes we were told where we could put our ruddy jumble sale. Often people ruffled our hair and asked us questions. At no stage did I feel threatened or awkward; I was doing a grown-up job and consequently was respected and important. That's the way it felt.

Needless to say, we boys were hugely competitive, arguing over whose heap was the biggest and who had the most interesting haul. Having collected a boot-full, we took ourselves back home to sift through it. Mum was happy for us to do this though it was pretty clear that we couldn't just keep anything we fancied. Not likely; it all had to go to the sale even if we might earmark something to buy on the day (of course, as foreshadowed above, that didn't apply to her!).

Once I was used as Mum's Artful Dodger. She had this thing about growing a variegated holly bush from a cutting so if ever she saw one, she was after a snippet; we lads were primed to tell her if we spotted one on our forays. The time in question, the owners were outside, gardening. Mum, for reasons that now aren't entirely clear, didn't want to ask them for a cutting (I suppose because they might have said no) so, while she distracted them, I was sent to break off a branch. Looking back, I suppose if I was caught she would have remonstrated with me and threatened some dire punishment. As it was, I managed to nab a piece of foliage - what Mum euphemistically called, if asked, "summer pruning", allowing her to pursue another attempt at cultivation.

On the night before the big sale we would drive to the church hall in Caterham and deposit all we had collected; others did the same, but I'm proud to say few outstripped the Le Pards' mountain of stuff. This process could well involve several carloads; while Mum and one son went back to collect another load, the remaining son joined in on the Great Sort. This, too, was fun, separating out various clothing items, household goods and, best of all, books. Toys too but really, books were the biggie. Often times we'd have started this process by the time Dad returned from work; he'd make his way to the hall to join in, usually to rousing cheers and jeers from his friends – "late again, Le Pard", "I see you're still slacking", "your wife can't do all the work in your family, can she?", "you even use your lads as slave labour". I think I understood the good nature of the banter even at my tender years.

At some point, because bedtimes were sacrosanct, we would be taken back home, bribed with something I expect, while one or other grandma would babysit. Mum and Dad would continue getting everything ready and then retire to the clubhouse for a few drinks and card games.

Saturday dawned bright and early (perhaps not for my parents – they were probably a little dusty after the night's imbibing – though they hid it well). This was a frantic day, when cash floats for the stalls had to be distributed, pricing instructions given, cakes produced etc.

The Archaeologist and I were always placed on the book stall. This was run not by a parent, but by a fearsome man who was a "bachelor" – which I now realise was to mean he was gay – called Geoffrey Spence. Geoffrey abhorred little boys, swore a lot and drank Danish lager by the bucket load – his house was called Tuborg Halt with a British Rail sign indicating same.

Over the several years that we two worked for Geoffrey on the book stall, he moaned at the imposition of free babysitting services that he provided, complained we were a liability and fulminated at having to stop us "giving away the Crown Jewels".

133

But my memories of him are of a twinkly-eyed gentleman, who loved the fact the Archaeologist read classics at the age of eight. He always found me something, that no one else had spotted that I would like, and, above all, he diligently ensured that no one took any advantage of us.

Doors opened at two pm prompt, and the unholy rush when they did took your breath away. Geoffrey would stand in front of our stall, with the Archaeologist and me behind it; as the first group approached he would glare at them and issue his Rules of Purchase in stentorian tones and then hand the buyers over to his assistants – us – who would be pleased to help with any queries. Sometimes he'd tut over something someone looked at – "trash" or "rubbish" might be mumbled under his breath. Sometimes he'd tell the prospective buyer that they couldn't possibly understand what they were looking at and to "bugger off". Generally, however, his presence and demeanour meant the whole sales business was conducted with some decorum.

Unlike over on clothing. Always the first customers through the door were a group of sharp beaked women; they would head for the piles of clothes and start pulling them onto the floor. The game, to which people got wise, was that, once on the floor, and out of sight of the people behind taking money and restocking the tables, these items would be swiftly stuffed into bags and, in the rhyming phrase of the time, "half-inched (pinched)".

Clothing was always carnage for the first hour and it was here Mum and one or two other formidable women were posted.

Dad? You know, I've no idea. I'd suspect he did committee things like circulate and offer his good wishes and gratitude – as Mum might say "he was a natural at the Lady Muck glad-handing". I suppose he worked a stall, but I was having too much fun to notice.

This shebang continued for three hours until people were ushered out at five pm. We were exhausted, but the world didn't stop here. Oh no. We had the money, and often we had the unsold items to take away too. Back home we'd go to count the change. To say life was simple would be an understatement, but a Saturday night confronted with the bucket loads of halfpennies and pennies, three-penny bits and florins; these were the stuff of dreams to this little boy. My hands turned black and my arms were sore, but we kept going until we finished.

If Dad could combine his love of Mum (and her garden) with a slight bit of showing off, he was never happier. I can imagine him grinning as she opened her card this particular year.

Historically Speaking...
(October 21 1998)

Old Adam was the first gardener,
Who spent many wearisome hours,
Working hard for his God,
Outside, on his tod,
Tending Eden's veg., fruit and flowers.
*

And so he was hugely relieved
When Eve arrived on the scene,
And soon she became
So skilled at the game
That he thought 'Her fingers are green!'
*

It has been like that ever since
And there isn't a shadow of doubt,
That, if we men fumble
We are soon looking humble,
When the girls get their secateurs out!
*

Down the years, famous lady gardeners,
Have become part of England's glory
Growing flowers and shrubs
In pots and tubs
On the ground – or on the top storey!
*

Men sometimes pack in when it's tough,
But the ladies have more staying power
They don't trust to luck
But with trowels, fork (and muck)
Get gardening -Behold! There's a flower!
*

I, more than most, know all this
And I am the first to agree

135

That, as in so much
My own 'dear old Dutch'
Is a far better gardener than me!
*

Horticulturally, she is a natural
And friends and the family know it,
If it won't root, or shoot,
Or bear any fruit,
Just give it to Barbara – she'll grow it!

Twenty-Nine

The Age Of Steam

I spent a large amount of my childhood in steam. Mum's kitchen was a cauldron of cooking and boiling. At most times of the year it seemed some industrial catering process was under way – marmalade, chutney, jam, preserving vegetables like beetroot – and when the smells weren't culinary they involved boiled clothing or some other mechanical process.

This was, you might understand, back when a vegetable was cooked to a pulp, or so it seemed. Cabbage wasn't eaten crisp, the only thing stir fried was a chip pushed around the pan and had we heard the term al dente we would have assumed it referred to an Italian dentist.

Mum used a pressure cooker a lot of the time, which generated both steam and a series of whizzes and fizzes that made her kitchen appear to be a prototype for a potions lesson.

Sometimes Mum could become a bit reckless. On one occasion she was trying to rush and had the heat turned up too high on the pressure cooker.

For those of you who have never experienced these marvels, they cooked whatever it was in pressurised steam, but as with all things under pressure there needed to be an escape; and in this case, there were weights on the top. Were the pressure to get to be too much and the neat little vent to prove insufficient, the weights would pop off the top and roll to one side letting all the steam out thus avoiding the pressure cooker from turning into shrapnel.

Unfortunately, in this instance, the weights didn't so much roll as rocket. One minute the kitchen was full of a low-level crackle, the next it was filled with an enormous pop. The weights hit the ceiling, as I tried desperately to exit stage right, screaming; Mum, who was in the process of pulling the complicated wooden contraption which was full of recently washed clothes, let go of the rope and everything fell to the floor, much to her annoyance; and the dog, twenty-seven kilos of muscle, proved once more that the only thing entirely frictionless in the known universe is a sprinting dog on wet linoleum.

If I escaped steam at one end of the house, I might well find it at the other. One year, the Archaeologist was given a small steam-powered engine. He was fascinated by many things and the power of steam was one. This little piece of engineering marvel – a Mamod – was a scale model of a working steam engine. It used a little burner fuelled with methylated spirits to heat the water.

Looking back, you do have to wonder at my parents and their gullibility, allowing an eight-year old Frankenstein loose with such inflammable material. They trusted him, which in one sense is meritorious. And really, if I'm being honest here, something that might be used to conflagrate the house was small beer to him.

This was the boy whose imagination was beyond his years. Somehow, all blue eyes, blond curls, to the fore, he persuaded Mum (and remember this was well before his tenth birthday) to buy him some saltpetre – potassium nitrate - because he wanted to do a small chemical experiment. Back then fertilizer bombs were a thing of sci-fi imaginings, not the staple of the internet and crazed terrorists, but they were not beyond the wide reading of the Archaeologist. Sourcing sulphur and charcoal wasn't tricky either, for one so duplicitous.

The small "accident" that occurred when he lit a metal dish with these compounds in it "to see how it went" led to a sooty mark on our bedroom ceiling and some melted sticky-backed plastic on our table. How this wasn't noticed is a mystery.

Eventually he managed to blow up a small amount of lawn – not telling anyone, of course – and there, we must be grateful his experiments in ordnance ended.

Neither of us thought there was anything wrong with this. He built a horn for an old-fashioned gramophone player using one of Mum's sewing needles; it ended up so deeply embedded in the heel of my foot that I required an operation to remove it. Did I want the experiments to stop? Hardly. A little collateral damage was a small price to pay to satiate for a while an otherwise unquenchable curiosity.

Would he be the polymath he is today had that urge been restrained? Maybe not. Anyway, I'm sure he's forgiven me now for breaking that needle given how long it took him to make that horn…

If Mum and Dad delighted in one thing in their later years it was having the grandchildren around. Dad would delight in taking them on muddy trips onto the Forest, letting them climb trees and bounce on decidedly dodgy peat bogs. He could spend hours encouraging in them both a fascination for nature and an understanding of how best to undermine their parents' authority. Meanwhile Mum would make everything a game and, if there were any creative urges needing to be fulfilled she was the one to do it. Food and imagination played a huge part in Mum's relationship with her four grandchildren. This poem comes from that love.

A Gardening Grandma

I have a wife who's a gardener,
And when I say that I don't mean
One who quivers and quails
When she sees slugs or snails,
And who can't tell a bulb from a bean!
*

But rather a down to earth lady
Who's aware that the plain, simple fact is
Success – IF it comes
Isn't due to 'green thumbs',
But hard work, knowledge and practice.
*

She'll grow the most difficult plant
By knowing just what it needs,
And when putting in order
An overgrown border,
She won't mix plantlets with weeds.
*

The weather never deters her,
She gardens in sunshine or shower,
And she's only put out
If we get a bad drought,
Then she'll water for hour after hour.
*

She knows how to nurse a sick tree
And coax a recalcitrant shrub,

139

She can ever repair
A cracked garden chair,
And make good an old broken tub.
*

She's made wooden archways and trellis,
And pyramids where climbers scramble
She's an angel in gloves
With plants that she loves,
But ruthless with bindweed and bramble.
*

The knowledge that she has acquired
Through the years is highly respected,
She's become quite well known
A fact which is shown
By the prizes and cups she's collected.
*

For her sacks of compost or leafmould
Are sources of infinite pleasure,
And the subtle allure
Of a load of manure
Far exceeds that of Solomon's Treasure!
*

As a Grandma she's in great demand,
For no-one is gentler or kinder,
And if when they shout
She seems to be out
The children known just where to find her.
*

And so Barbara picks up her trug,
And wearing her jerkin and gloves
With a song in her heart
And eager to start
Steps into the garden she loves.

Thirty

Sleeping Through A Crisis

I have inherited a number of traits from Mum: her patience (at least I like to think so); her instinct for cooking without a recipe; and, above all, her optimism and refusal to be down for long. But one that has both served me well and caused me untold embarrassment is the ability to fall asleep pretty much anywhere. The "power nap" is definitely in the genes.

Mostly, this is harmless (if not undertaken while using machinery of any kind). But it can frustrate other people. And I certainly had an early example of its aggravating side while learning an important life lesson from Mum.

It all began at primary school, when a new teacher decided to introduce us to Scottish country dancing.

Mrs Greening, in what would now be called year four, taught us the eponymous gyrations. Having had to suffer years of Music and Movement when vigorous little bodies were expected to imitate a petal falling in autumn at the point where their repertoire solely comprised an approximation of an ICBM hurtling towards Moscow, it was a welcome change.

Until, that is, one day when I ricked my neck performing a rather epic, if less than traditional, Stripping the Willow.

Boy, do I remember that. The pain was awful, every movement sending shoots of fire across my shoulders and down my side. The treatment was manipulation followed by a deep heating of the affected area courtesy of an enormous infrared lamp. It was bloody medieval, people. However, the worst bit turned out to be my caring parent, Mum. She accompanied me, as you'd expect her to do. She understood my distress and loaded her bag with some sweets (an unaccustomed treat) and the latest Famous Five book I was reading so she could distract me with it as I fried.

So far so marvellous.

We were taken to an empty ward which, had I been older and more familiar with horror films, might have been creepy, but I was a compliant boy so did as I was told. The nurse, from memory, had on one of those oddly starched uniforms that suggested it was made from crispbread. She must have given brusque instructions because, in next to no time, with my mother, happily it seemed, going along with all the Tartar said, a solar lamp had been wheeled next to a bed and I was strapped into this stretching machine. Quite literally. A strap was placed under my jaw and another round my ankles and the ends were tied to rollers. Slowly the nurse turned the handles until the straps were tight and I was completely held in place.

Did my neck hurt? I guess, but since my mouth had been so forcibly closed by this oddly inquisitional instrument, I couldn't have said.

'I'll come back and check on you (a cruel euphemism I soon learned stood for "I will tighten this torture machine") in twenty minutes.'

Mum patted me on the shoulder, watching my expression for signs of distress. Have you ever been held immobile by the jaw? It is a sort of reverse Botox with every facial muscle squeezed into its neighbour, wrinkle forced on top of wrinkle. I could no more have registered happy or sad as I could have whistled for my supper.

The only saving grace was I was going to be read to; at least that would distract me. For five minutes Mum set the scene with George, Tim and Anne and the rest of the Five and then she dropped off to sleep. Deeply. Sonorously. Could I wake her? With my jaw strapped and my feet tied? Hardly. I lay there, until the nurse came and tightened my straps. Mum bounced awake trying and failing to look as if she had been conscious throughout.

'How's he doing?' the nurse asked.

'Fine. Not a peep.'

'Grand.'

They exchanged smiles, Mum settled, yawned and promptly nodded off again.

I learnt a salutary lesson that day: however loving a parent, however intent on being a comfort and support, combine a warm fug with a good book and they will go to sleep. It's as hard-wired as the flight or fight instinct. Now that I am a parent myself, I understand why...

This is the second of Dad's major epic Forest poems which he had published in a Forest magazine. He was proud of this like no other, I think and worked on it pretty constantly, seeking out improved meters and rhymes.

The Old Road
(A Tale Of The New Forest)

It is said that civilisation is only a thin veneer,
And just a crack in the surface can uncover a well of fear,
A morass of superstition, where reason is put to rout,
And comfortable, clear convictions degenerate into doubt.
*

Four of us boarded the local stage at the 'Angel' in Lymington Town,
With Coachman John that made five souls, all of us Ringwood bound,
And the cheerful chatter and bustle as the coach prepared to leave,
Was enriched by a note of revelry, for was this not New Year's Eve?
*

In the Year of Our Lord 1815, a time of England's might,
When Wellington, at Waterloo, had shown how Englishmen fight,
And healed, with that great victory, the nation's running sore,
By bringing peace to the people, after weary years of war.
*

No Christmastide had ever seen more wassail and goodwill,
And the poorest in the parishes for once had fed their fill,
For the Mayor himself had made it known that joy should come to all,
And even the Frenchy prisoners had danced at the Yuletide Ball.
*

But that day we four good citizens, merchants of some renown,
Were travelling to Ringwood, to dine that night at the 'Crown',
Meanwhile, to keep out the bitter cold, we had cracked a bottle or two,
While Coachman John had supped right well on the 'Angel's' famed
home brew.
*

'Come, gentlemen all,' called Coachman John, 'tis time for us to go,'
'The wind has turned, it's due nor'east, and I don't doubt it will snow.'
We hurried then, though we were loath to leave the fireside bright,
For we were aware that the Forest was no place to be snowbound at
night.

143

Though John had a brace of pistols and each of us wore a sword
And none of us was a coward, yet we knew there roamed abroad
Desperate and dangerous rogues, vagabonds, thieves – and worse,
Who would slit the throat of an honest man for the guineas in his
purse.
*

The wind, as we hastened across the yard, was razor-sharp and raw,
And its icy fingers froze the flesh through the thick coats that we wore.
The coach-springs squeaked as we climbed aboard and huddled in our
seats,
With blankets wrapped around us and hot bricks at hands and feet.
*

John swiftly mounted the driving-box, felt the bite of the wind and
swore.
Then grinned at a buxom serving-wench, 'You'd keep me warm for
sure!'
The ostlers let go the horses' heads and the coach, with a jolt and a
lurch,
Moved forward though the 'Angel's' arch and swung right towards the
church.
*

Through the town we drove at spanking pace and soon we could espy
The high, bare mounds of Buckland Rings, stark against the sky,
While lower down the great reed beds stood drowning in the flood
Which well-nigh every winter makes our water-meadows mud.
*

I looked at my companions, men I'd known all my life,
The Manson brothers, Paul and Hugh, whose sister was my wife,
And whose good Forest timber, oaken planking from their yard,
Was part of every man-o'-war launched from Buckler's Hard.
*

Beside me, Martin Johnson, late of the Fusiliers,
Who had gallantly campaigned, unscathed, for nearly fifteen years,
'Til the sabre of a French Hussar, south of Salamanca,
Had sent him home and changed his rank, from brigadier to banker.
*

But the wine we'd drunk in our merry mood was strong, and talk soon
lagged,

And eyelids drooped as the coach rolled on, and on four chests four chins sagged,
And none of us noticed the first snowflakes, soft and white as they swirled,
For as John pulled out onto Setley Plain we were sleeping, and dead to the world.

*

How long I slept I cannot say – I awoke with a violent start,
And the certainty that something was wrong, and a pounding in my heart,
While all around was a curious light, a strangely luminous glow,
Which revealed my three companions and, dim, through the window, snow.

*

Martin Johnson and the Mansons lay sprawled out, still fast asleep,
And it seemed to me uncanny that their slumber should be so deep
For surely what had awakened me should have aroused them, too,
And I shouted as I shook each one, 'Wake up, Martin, Paul, Hugh!'

*

There was no response, I thought they were dead – then I saw, thank God, I was wrong,
By the regular movement of each man's chest as he breathed steady and strong,
But their features were still and lifeless, as though carved out of stone,
And I knew that whatever lay ahead I would have to face alone.

*

I climbed from the coach into a world snowbound, silent and still,
The weird light illuminated all, and I recognised Wilverley Hill,
Across the valley Wooton sloped, and I knew, though I peered in vain,
That far ahead the turnpike ran, in the shadow of Goatspen Plain.

*

As a boy I'd explored this countryside on my Forest pony's back,
I'd forded the streams and skirted the bogs and climbed every hill and track,
I'd known where the otter took his trout, and the honey buzzard flew,
I'd seen badger cubs playing by moonlight and followed the fox through the dew.

*

I'd walked in the deep inclosures by the charcoal-burners hut,
And, on quiet October evenings, heard the red deer roar at rut,

145

I'd skated over Hatchett Pond, and laughed as the summer rain
Spangled the hair of the gipsy maid who I'd kissed on Red Shoot Plain.
*

I'd welcomed the wild December gales when they raged in from the
sea,
And watched the great oaks writhe and twist and bow to their mastery,
I loved this Forest in all its moods, and I'd learned its secret ways,
And it had been playground and schoolroom since my earliest
childhood days.
*

But the Forest this night, as I stood alone, was an awful, alien place,
With features entirely familiar – but wearing no friendly face,
But breathing a brooding menace, an evil malignant air,
And I felt a numbing helplessness, like a rabbit in a snare.
*

I looked up at Coachman John, that big man, bluff and brave,
And I saw how he sat on his driving-box, like a statue over a grave,
Shoulders hunched in a caped topcoat, tricorne rammed low on his
head,
While his thick-gloved hands held the reins to horses as still as the
dead.
*

Frightened, alone, in that frozen world, above all I craved human
speech,
When the silence was violently ripped apart by an eldritch screech
Shocked, I staggered against the coach while beneath my feet the
ground
Shook and trembled and rumbled – then again that unearthly sound.
*

I saw a huge black form rush by, belching fire and smoke,
The stench was foul and sulphurous and I thought that I would choke,
But though I smelt its acrid breath, I even then knew well
That this was not some demon, or fiery hound from Hell.
*

No pale apparition this, sad fruit of an unhinged mind,
But something hard and tangible which was drawing close behind
Several great wheeled boxes, each one filled with light,
And thundering by in line, almost snakelike in the night.
*

With senses reeling I half fell, my body could stand no more,

146

And stumbling to the coach I clambered back in through the door,
I was drained of any courage, trembling weakly, and I wept,
I collapsed back in my seat, closed my aching eyes, and slept.
*

Then I heard Martin's laughter and saw him pretend to frown,
'Come, wake up, you old rogue, we are nearing Ringwood Town!'
'And tell us, pray, what was your dream while you slumbered long and
deep?'
'For you have kept us all awake, muttering in your sleep!'
*

But how could I answer his question? And who, indeed, would believe
Such an unlikely take – especially on New Year's Eve?
But I know something happened out there in that curious light,
And I see it all as clear today as I did on that far-off night.
|*

I've made that journey many times, and always I tense in my seat
As we reach the place, and I live it again, and feel my heart miss a
beat,
And you ask why a sensible man like me trembles with foolish fear?
Well, they say common sense, like civilisation is only a thin veneer!

Historical note: The Southampton and Dorchester railway (now long
defunct) opened in 1847, some thirty-two years after the above events
occurred, and the track across the New Forest is believed by some to
have followed part of the old Lymington to Ringwood stagecoach
road.

Thirty-One

Weather To Forgive

Learning lessons from Mum took many guises. There were obvious ones, spelt out in an English I could understand and maybe reinforced with a threat (never idle) or a bribe. There were others that appeared unexpectedly but which have resonated ever since. This one involves the weather.

It wasn't always sunny when I was a child. My memory is not that simplistic. Yes, I remember sunny days – one especially sticks out when I sat down in some long grass and found a broken milk bottle by the expedient of lacerating my bum. I was maybe six. It was horrendous, but my parents for ever after told me I was very brave – I suspect now it was to try and assuage the guilt they felt as the doctor probed the wound to see if any glass was left inside. Whatever, it hurt to all buggery and started me on my collection of stitches that down the years have easily topped one hundred.

No, there are two climatic moments that really stick out.

First is the winter of 1962/63 and especially the period around February when we had snow for a month or more. School shut regularly and Mum pulled the Archaeologist and me to the shops on a toboggan. I think that was the first, maybe only time, when I really really didn't want any more snow. Now it is so rare it is a treat to see, even with the chaos that ensues. Or it means I've gone skiing which is a not so secret pleasure. Mum never really "got" snow, I think because of the damage it did to her plants. Frost could be necessary as part of nature's way of ensuring the required level of hibernation and restoration, but snow was for other countries, thank you very much.

The other is rain and one especially heavy and continuous downpour. I loved downpours. Not drizzle or brief pulses, but proper old-fashioned "it's set in for the day" rain. This one lasted more than a day – some time in the mid-1960s I guess. We lived in a cul-de-sac called Anne's Walk which was at the very top of a hill. Goodness, did we get hit with the weather up there.

Our house sat at the end of a steepish slope and when it rained, the water ran away down the gutters at a fair old rate. In my memory I had caught the bus from school and was on my own – maybe the

Archaeologist had started secondary school by then which would place it about 1967, and I was already drenched when I got on the bus.

A few of us alighted at the same stop, chatting before we made our ways to our homes; this day everyone scattered to miss the rain. Except me. I stood in what was a warm continuous shower with no one else outdoors – perhaps that is what made it perfect, the lack of anyone else, especially adults.

I took my time walking from the bus stop to our turning, which took me up that slope. I stopped and stared. I can see it now; the rain was no longer confined to the gutters; it had crossed the road, easily defeating the camber and had created a river between the pavements. It was beginning to crest the top of the far gutter and spill out and over the pavement into the garden next to it. Twigs and summer leaves, dislodged by this deluge, hurtled past me, recklessly sweeping out of our road with complete disregard to the "Look left, right and left again" admonishments to which I was subjected.

Had I known of tsunamis I might have thought this was one, so extraordinary it was. A car went past the junction, its wheels churning through the water throwing sheets across the windows and obscuring the driver.

And despite the fact my skin was wet, my clothes losing their traction and slipping off me, I was warm and happy. It was bliss.

I danced up through the deepest water and back down and up again, three or four times. My school sandals – it was the summer term and my brown sandals were part of the school uniform alongside grey shorts, a grey cotton shirt and a black and yellow diagonally striped tie – were barely staying on my feet. My socks were so full of water that they had wrapped themselves round my shoes. I had a raincoat on – ha! joke – which had somehow become tangled around me.

The words like "saturated" don't do justice to my state. I didn't want that walk home to end.

It was only as I left our road and turned into the short drive alongside our house that the reality of my condition began to create a sense of apprehension. Even I, as young as I was, was aware that my whole uniform was no longer fit for purpose, yet I would need it the next day. I also knew, with something akin to a sickening certainty, that going indoors as wet as I was, was not going to add to my naturally endearing personality.

I approached our front door and wondered at Mum's reaction. She could be tough - ruthless even – and having her afternoon thrown out by the need to correct my attempts to become aquatic would have tried her patience.

I knocked and waited to be let in, somewhat tremulous.

I can see her now, appraising me. Not a long appraisal before, glory be, she began to laugh. She laughed fit to bust. She said, afterwards, that I looked so happy she couldn't be cross. Mind you she made me strip off every stitch of clothing in the hall which was acutely embarrassing so she had some retribution.

Mum always spoke of my love of rain and reminded me of this when we watched her grandson dancing around her garden – by then he was six or so – just to enjoy the simple delights of the pouring rain. 'I loved rain, too. It must be in the genes.'

I hope so; that and her laughter at the absurdity of small boys and downpours.

I've said Dad did rather focus on age, in his more public poems, this being one.

The Wrinkles Lament

When we gaze in the mirror while shaving
We mustn't get too uptight,
Though the sight makes us weep
Beauty's only skin deep,
And we're bound to look better tonight.
*

Sparse locks on an over-wide forehead
Where once clustered nonchalant curls,
If dissuaded from roaming
By judicious combing
Just might deceive short-sighted girls.
*

We've always had finely drawn features
But the nostrils in that Roman beak
Which in wild youth would flare
Are now full of hair,
And constantly saltily leak.
*

Our eyes, which held love's sweet secrets,
Were mysterious, soft – dark as night,
Now they're bloodshot and runny
And one's a bit funny,
Looking left when the other looks right.
*

These firm chiselled mouths show good breeding
But today they can spoil our adventures
For though you feel sporty
It's hard to be naughty
If you find you've forgotten your dentures.
*

Girlish breath in the ear was exciting
In our youth, we recall with nostalgia,
But now, poor old mugs,
If you blow down our lugs,

151

We'll get an attack of neuralgia.
*

But it's wrong to become introspective
That mirror can ruin our fun,
Let's stop shaving today
Chuck our razors away
Grow beards – and think we're twenty-one!

Thirty-Two

The Logic Of Pets

One more life lesson, about love. We had pets, comprising a much-loved dog, a rabbit found running loose in a Surrey wood and, after I'd moved to London, a cat called Misty. But these were family pets, not "mine" in any sense. Not until I was gifted a guinea pig one birthday.

She was Gertie; history no longer relates from whence that name came. She was a mix of light browns and white, seemingly an inch deep in fur and as indolent as any cherry tree on a sunny sultry spring day. She allowed herself to be held but failed to reciprocate the affection I was prepared to shower on her. She tolerated the handling as she continued gurning and cud chewing her jaw, on and on like her teeth didn't fit properly. She took cucumber from me with a supercilious air. It felt a little like being granted an audience. She might be a rodent, but she was a blue-blooded one.

As is the way with pet maintenance for the young, the enthusiasm wanes when the hard yards are required. I would have been happy to ignore the regular cage cleaning that is needed but for Mum. She saw a life lesson, ready to be played out, and I was cajoled, bribed and entreated to "look after" my pet, as otherwise she would "have to go".

This awful balance caused me a lot of angst: on one side I loved the idea of this living thing being "mine"; on the other the regular proximity of my fingers to guinea pig faeces put that love under intense strain.

I'm sure I made no fuss; I can say that because (a) no one is here to challenge it and (b) if there was one thing Mum never tolerated it was whinging, it was a crime requiring severe retribution, along with littering and someone appearing at the front door trying to sell her a religion when she was cooking.

In truth, from the point Gertie appeared, our relationship followed a fairly steady downwards curve until one day she escaped. I imagine I failed to latch her hutch correctly – it's the sort of thing I'd do. But her bid for freedom didn't take into account the other mammal that shared our house at the time.

This was the family dog, a boxer called Punch. He was big and drooly and wouldn't really hurt a fly. Except Her Royal Ratness didn't

153

know that. When Gertie, no doubt perambulating slowly and taking in the new surroundings, found herself swept up inside the Jaws of Hell she didn't immediately think "let's play". Rather I imagine it was nearer "What the fuck?"

The squealing was horrendous, reaching a pitch that made nails on blackboards seem soothing in comparison. Mum managed to rescue her, physically unharmed but psychologically scarred. She (Gertie, not Mum) developed a twitch. She became prone to RABs – random acts of biting – and she began to fade. I am sorry to say that when eventually she died I didn't mourn her passing.

No, looking back, I realised that, in truth, I was with Punch. What I wanted was a playmate. I had gained a sentient warm-blooded toy, not a reciprocating friend. I can't be certain, but my affections for our daft dog grew after Gertie's demise. Mum was the same; always a dog for her. Well, until the cat appeared to take over her heart...

My parents had one pet, after our much-loved boxer died. Misty, a small and hardy tabby cat that brought many shrews and mice into the house, often dropping them into Dad's shoes and boots.

Misty

Our Misty is an English cat
Whose natural feline grace
Conceals inside a haughty pride
In her native English race
*

Her sire sprang from New Forest stock
And her dam from a Midland shire
And she was born on St George's morn
In the warmth of a Hampshire byre.
*

On her mother's side, generations gone,
Cats more wild than tame
Saw Royalists yield on Naseby field,
Cursing the Roundhead name.
*

And earlier yet her father's kin,
Of the Wessex woodland race,
Watched an arrow fly, saw the Red King die,
And Tyrrell fall from grace.
*

The law of the countryside she knows,
As a kitten the lesson was learned,
That to live and thrive, to stay alive,
Is a privilege hard-earned.
*

She knows this land on warm summer nights,
She has hunted through the snow,
She has heard the trees sing their symphonies
When the great south-westers blow.
*

And now, on this black November night,
I doze by my fireside warm,
While the windowpane is lashed with rain

Of our first real winter storm.

*

Down at my feet our Misty lies,
Silent, she slumbers on,
What dreams are hers? Ears twitch, she stirs,
Stands, stretches – and is gone.

Thirty-Three

The Surveillance Society, New Milton Branch

My mother was eighty-one when she moved into her new bungalow. Her long overdue knee replacement, while removing the discomfort, did not increase her inclination to exercise. Never one to do anything that might be considered "good" for you if it didn't fit her own current idea of what was "good", she wasn't especially mobile. In designing the refurbishment, I managed to persuade her to have a wet room installed which, despite reservations, she loved. No steps into the shower and a seat to perch on as she abluted. 'Yes, darling, it has been a good move.'

If that was a plus, the other item I persuaded her to include was less successful. The video entrance system. The concept was, of course, simple and the technology well-tried and tested. From the start she didn't like it, especially as there were teething problems around the day of her move.

Several times I would be regaled with tales of the difficulties faced by people who had come to the front door, the problems, almost inevitably it seemed, being tied into the new system.

'I really didn't like his attitude. He wouldn't look at the camera.'

'It's stopped working altogether. Waste of money. I expect it's German.'

This last comment came some six months after she moved in. I promised to look at it on my next visit. When I asked her to describe the problem, she told me she couldn't hear what the visitor was saying. And she couldn't see the visitors at all.

On the sound issue I did wonder if this was because of her reluctance to use her deaf aids when not "in company". I checked and I couldn't hear anything either. It took no time to realise this was because the volume was turned right down. Odd. It wasn't as if anyone could easily knock it and accidentally reduce the volume. I asked Mum. 'I need to lean in close and when I do it makes my deaf aid fizz. After I fiddled with it the fizz went.' As did the sound.

Feedback. I spoke to the company and they started by suggesting I tell my mother to stand further away. I explained that wasn't an optimal solution so in the end they agreed they would send someone to try to sort it out.

As for the picture, the camera had been moved so it pointed down rather than ahead. At best Mum could tell if the visitor was wearing brogues or trainers; given her snobbery that might in fact have been more helpful for her.

I adjusted it and showed Mum how it looked. She nodded but remained non-committal as to whether she was now satisfied.

The next time we spoke the technician had visited.

'How is the video entry now?'

'The man sorted out the feedback. He suggested I just need to stand back a little or get them to speak up. I'm surprised they didn't tell you that. It would have saved him a journey. He lives in Romsey and had to defibrillate his clutch.'

'Defibrillate? Isn't that something to do with the heart?'

'He was lovely.' That ended that conversation; he could do no wrong.

'And the picture?'

'Oh that. It's gone again. I think the camera must be loose.'

Well, at least she had sound. I'd sort the camera out next time, see if I could fix it in place. Better than call out another technician and be accused, by her, of wasting his time.

I couldn't find any sign the camera was loose so readjusted it and suggested that Mum try and avoid touching it (I assumed that, perhaps, her cleaner might be moving it accidentally).

A couple of weeks on and, unusually, I was down at Mum's on a weekday. The doorbell went; Mum was in the hall so was nearest the front door. I stood by the kitchen door, drying my hands. To my surprise, rather than pressing the video button to see who it was, Mum immediately opened the door. It looked like a utility man.

She reached round to where the camera sat and said, 'You need to speak up. In there.' It looked like she tapped the camera. 'And speak clearly.'

She closed the door and, only then, did she press the intercom button. 'Yes? Who is it?'

The surprise in the utility man's voice was apparent. 'Gas, madam.'

'The meter is round the side. Thank you.'

Mum turned to face me. 'What are you laughing at?'

'Do you really do that for all visitors or was that just to show me how useless my idea was?'

She, maybe, grinned a little as she walked past me. 'Don't be silly, darling. If I knew who it was I wouldn't close the door on them, would I? It could have been electric and he would need to come in to access to his meter. Tea? Orange polenta cake?'

I stopped wondering too hard about the droopy camera; Mum wasn't taking the intercom seriously after all so it hardly mattered. But every time I visited I took a moment to adjust the camera to the right position.

One day, months later, we went out, to a garden centre and bought some bags of topsoil or compost. So, unusually, Mum went to the front door to let herself in while I pulled the bags from the boot. Normally, as a well-trained young man, I would have done the door opening bit.

Something made me watch. Maybe I just wanted to make sure she was safe inside; her mobility issues made her unsteady at times. As usual, I had fixed the camera on my arrival the day before.

As she approached the door she rummaged for her keys. She pulled them out and looked up. Even though her back was to me I knew what that depression of the shoulders meant: disapproval at something. She reached out with her free hand and pressed on the entrance camera before opening the door.

When I got inside I asked about what she'd done.

'It's awful. That mirror thingy makes me look like Ken Dodd after he's done his tax return. I just moved it a little.'

'So, you move it?'

'Of course.'

'You know that's why the camera only shows the visitor's shoes?'

'Darling, it's bad enough seeing myself in that thing, but I can't have my friends being forced to go through that. They'll think I can see them looking all distorted when they come to the front door. It might work with your friends but, really, it's simply not on.'

The next year, when the renewal contract came in, we filed it under "pending". It remained pending.

Another Birthday poem.

The Gardener, October 21 1999

Barbara's a natural gardener,
Possessing 'green thumbs' as they say,
And her cuttings thrive
And all stay alive,
While frequently mine fade away!
*

Her enthusiasm is boundless,
The garden's her passion and pride,
So while in a storm
We seek to keep warm,
She prefers being outside.
*

For our weather's not always clement,
We get rain and, occasionally, snow,
But though the day's foul
With fork, trug and trowel
Out in the garden she'll go.
*

When we visit the Saturday market
The clothes shops don't give her a thrill,
The best thing of all
Is her favourite stall
Run by George, on Lymington Hill.
*

She prefers garden centres for shopping,
And her idea of a treat
Is to wander for hours
Round the shrubs and the flowers,
Then come home with a large bag of peat.
*

Over the years in the garden,
She's developed ideas by the score,
And I know, in her heart,
That for her the best part
Is ringing the changes once more.

160

Her garden will never be boring,
If something's too bland out it goes!
And this year's fresh sight
Which affords huge delight
Is her scarecrow with long pointed nose!
*

She's made me a 'butterfly border',
Planted with much skill and care,
And on warm, sunny days
I've loved to just gaze
On the bees and the butterflies there.
*

When Barbara announces at breakfast,
'The house is in such disarray'
'I feel quite ashamed,'
'Only I can be blamed,'
We know she'll go gardening today.
*

But we who know her and love her
Would have her no other way,
And we all gently smile
When she says, 'I think I'll'
'Really have to go gardening today.'

Thirty-Four

Taking Flight

While my mother was a determined and constantly busy person, she begrudged having to do any more walking than absolutely necessary. If Mark Twain thought golf ruined a good walk, Mum rather thought a "good walk" a bit of an oxymoron. After her long-delayed knee replacement and without Dad's constant nagging she took her rehabilitation somewhat half-heartedly and reduced her walking to a trickle. Indeed, I found out at one point, she was driving her rubbish from her backdoor to her dustbins at the end of her drive (we aren't talking Downton Abbey) rather than wheel the bins back and forth. When I expressed my surprise, and suggested that the exercise of wheeling a bin might be a good way to utilise her new knee, she reluctantly agreed. Next time I visited, the bins had been installed permanently at the end of the drive and she carried the rubbish bags to them by way of a second-hand golf trolley (sans bag) that she bought in Oxfam for a couple of quid.

There were some historic reasons for this antipathy which never affected the rest of us; at a relatively young age, in her early forties, she was diagnosed with rheumatoid arthritis. Back then, in the 1960s, this was expected to be crippling, but she was offered some fairly experimental drugs to try and moderate the impact. It did mean that walking could be excruciating for her and stairs an especial challenge. Mind you, garden centres and places like Sissinghurst and Hidcote never seemed as difficult.

There were side effects, especially in terms of her blood pressure. That in turn led to Mum having to forswear alcohol, something she begrudged more than having to walk.

Dad pretended to be sorry for her, but with the increasing pressure on stopping drinking and driving, he wasn't averse to the sober driver being Mum. Indeed, so commonplace was Dad driving to an event and Mum driving home that, when latterly in their marriage, the medication changed and she was told she could partake of the odd G&T or glass of wine, he found the idea that he was the one to stay "dry" hard to take.

'Des, you know you're driving tonight?'
'What? Are you sure?'

'Yes, it's your turn.'

'You sure you want to drink? You have to be careful.'

'Of course.'

'So, if you have, say, just a glass, then you could drive?'

The man was ever hopeful. Mum's reaction? A smile and a small shake of the head. Some people need to be loud in making their point. Not Mum. Her gestures tended to be minimalist, almost invisible but, for those who knew her, they spoke volumes. She knew her mind and didn't feel the need to ram any point home.

We all knew it was futile to assume she was deferring to us. A disinclination to debate might be capitulation in some but, with Mum, it was merely that there was no point wasting energy when the point was hers come what may. This manifested itself, once again, in how she dealt with her increasingly immobility.

During a regular call, she mentioned how the stairs to her bedroom were becoming more of a chore. We both knew or, at least, we both could guess, that because she had not followed the physiotherapist's programme post-knee replacement (and was unlikely to start now), she would need an alternative strategy.

And, indeed, when she bought her bungalow and had it refitted, this was included in the plans. We discussed it at some length. The dining room had been adapted so there was an ensuite wet room off it, which meant it could easily be converted to a downstairs bedroom if the need arose. As now. So, having posed the issue, Mum asked for my opinion on the most obvious solution.

'I guess we convert the dining room. As planned. You'll need to decide if you move your bed down there and maybe move out one or two bookcases or get a single bed for it.'

The dining room was lined with bookcases to create a library effect which she liked, but it did rather shrink the available space. I carried on, 'I suppose you may want to think about curtains – they're not blackout like in your bedroom - and whether...' I petered out. 'Mum, are you there?'

Something told me she wasn't engaging in my suggestions.

Still silence.

'Mum?'

'Your father would have liked the library. He always wanted one.'

You need to remember that, when my mother referenced my father, it wasn't because she was lost in memories or indulging in some maudlin reminiscence but rather as a sign that I was on the wrong track. So, thinking quickly, I realised she wanted to keep the library as it was which would mean a single bed. Even then it would be difficult for her to have a wardrobe downstairs. 'I suppose we could change the cupboard under the stairs, make it a small wardrobe. But then...'

'I like my bedroom, dear. It's lovely to look out over the garden.'

That threw me. 'Yes, but if the stairs are proving to be a challenge we need...'

'I thought a lift.'

Now this was a turn up. If Mum had ever commented on a stairlift, it wasn't in complimentary terms. 'Really? Okay. Well, if you think so? I can talk to a couple of the providers, find out what they can do and the sort of prices and...'

'A nice young man (another hint that she was ahead of me) came round last week. It will be a bit of a technical challenge, but he was sure they could sort it out.'

'Right? Who...? When...?'

'They're called Stannah. Dorothy (one of her WI stalwarts) raves about hers. The grandchildren love it.'

'Oh. Yes, well. Marvellous. Do you want me to talk to him, find out what...?'

'I just wondered if you wanted to be here when they fit it? They say it will be ready in about four weeks from now.'

You couldn't help smiling; she had it all sorted out and she played me like a rather dopey carp. Dad would have huffed and puffed, would have wanted to get competitive quotes and, in his last few years, debated things with me and the Archaeologist. She was well aware that when he knew he was dying, he impressed on me and the Archaeologist that we had to look after Mum (as if it needed saying, though he wasn't saying it for us but for Mum, the subliminal message being "Barbara, your sons will help you if you listen to them".) And the stages we went through that afternoon were a ritualised dance that was playing to his memory rather than any inclination Mum had to discuss something as mundane as a stairlift with me. Yes, she was saying, I know you can help but (a) I don't want to bother you; and (b) I'll ask for help when I need it; but (c) just in case he's still listening, let's pretend that I've consulted you.

The lift proved to be a success. She loved it, regally disappearing upstairs with a tray on her lap with whatever she needed. To my knowledge it never let her down and enabled her to spend her nights in her bedroom, at least until her final few weeks. And yes, it was appreciated by great-nieces, nephews and grandchildren. For her it was never per ardua, ad astra – through hard work we reach the stars – as much as per Stannah ad astra - by using a stairlift we'll get to bed; after all, Mum was never one for any sort of ardua if she could avoid it.

As I watched her disappear round the corner before she dismounted, I speculated on whether, had Dad been the surviving parent, he would have had a stairlift. No, I decided, he would have converted the dining room. He would have said it was because of cost, but really it would have been because he wanted to hide any frailty. Oddly, it was Mum's ability to embrace her weaknesses that made her the stronger of the two. How often is that true?

Dad's love of the insect world was a theme throughout his life and he became a real expert. His enjoyment of breeding them through and then letting them go grew with the years and I'm certain that, in his own modest way, he did a lot to hold back the tide of destruction that has swept through the ranks of the insect world in his last few years. This is the one poem I've found specifically on his passion.

A 'Dark' Decision
(Or Not To Be Taken 'Light'ly)

When Moths and Butterflies came on the scene
The world was still very young,
There was no pollution, it was all very clean,
And spring had only just sprung.
*

There hadn't been time for all of the flowers
To blossom and bloom in the sun,
But the Moths and the Butterflies spent hours and hours
Trying to visit each one.
*

They fluttered and flittered throughout the day
Every one of them, both large and small,
And soon they were getting in each other's way.
Said a Moth, 'This won't do at all.'
*

'We really must try and sort something out'
'Or there'll be a most horrible fight'
'The answer is clear – and I have no doubt'
'That someone must just fly at night!'
*

Fly at night! Fly at Night! What a ghastly idea!
Every antenna shook with alarm,
While thousands of wings quivered wildly with fear.
Said the Moth, 'Steady on, there – stay calm.'
*

'It only means we'll fly in the dark,'
'And for we insects that's no big deal'
'We can still find the flowers, quietly fly down and park'
'Then enjoy a leisurely meal.'

166

*

But the others still argued, and shouted out loud,
In fact, there was nearly a riot,
When a wise old Butterfly flew out from the crowd
Raised a wing, and bellowed for quiet.

*

'It's the only solution,' the Butterfly said,
'And we've got no choice but to try it'
'Because if we don't we'll starve – we'll be dead!'
'You're right,' said the crowd, 'So, we'll buy it.'

*

And that's what they did, and so from that day
All Butterflies have been DIURNAL,
But it's a sad fact, and I'm sorry to say
That not every moth is NOCTURNAL.

*

For there were some Moths who refused to agree,
Who insisted, 'We won't change! No Way!'
Which is why nowadays we frequently see
Several species still flying by day.

Thirty-Five

Landed Estate

My mother loved her garden. I don't think I can say this often enough. The family home in Hampshire morphed from an awful clay pit with a few decrepit fruit trees into a beautiful oasis. My parents put extraordinary effort into the conversion. Fortunately, their skills were complementary: Mum designed - she had the eye, the sense of scale and colour; Dad the passion and drive - he believed in the inevitability of the ultimate success and celebrated each small and large step with gusto. Indeed, little happened of a positive hue without a tipple being imbibed to mark such occasions. "Imbibing" was more than a pleasant adjunct to success; it was at the centre.

When Mum left Silver Crest after thirty-seven years, it was the leaving of the garden that took the most decoupling. Happily, the new bungalow had a garden though immediately I foresaw a problem. Mum was past eighty. She'd had a hip and knee replaced. She shared her joints with arthritis for years. It would be customary to say she "battled" these ailments, but Mum didn't really battle anything. She assessed her enemy and her wider resources and determined how to maximise her enjoyment of life with the minimum of personal engagement with the troubling parts.

An example: Dad's cancer made it difficult for him to walk far in the early day of his treatment. He was a walker and this was a major issue for him. When the Archaeologist and I took them to the Eden Project for what was likely to be our last holiday together as a foursome, I pre-booked wheelchairs for them both. Dad loathed the idea, bemoaning the loss of dignity, the inevitability he would be treated differently, the embarrassment. Mum only saw an opportunity to see more, for longer, and in more comfort. We, the packhorses, were to regret Mum's patent enthusiasm for being pushed - the Eden Project is bloody hilly. Eventually Dad saw what Mum had anticipated and embraced the experience - even exhorting me to "go faster, boy, they're getting away".

So, the new garden. It was largely lawn with a small bed to one side, a line of shrubs two thirds the way towards the back and a working area behind. Even on the day we moved her in, when I was still, forlornly, trying to negotiate some reduction on the amount of "stuff" we were squeezing into her new home, she was outside, casting a beady eye over her new empire.

'We need to change that bed.'

'We?' Of course, I knew. And she knew I knew.

'First you might tidy up the back, just to give me some space.' She gave me what might be described as an enigmatic look, but only if you've not lived with it for some forty years. It's a look that is waiting for the rubber stamp of acceptance, a look that says, "you can say no, of course you can, but is that what you really want, is that wise?" The tilt of the head, the glint of the glasses, the slow dawning of a smile and then, 'I'll make you some scones; I've some of the lemon curd saved somewhere.'

Frankly it was too big for her.

Sadly, I couldn't do as much for her as I wanted so we found a gardener; a wonderfully dynamic, energetic dash of a woman call Kath who ran super marathons and brought the same fizz and endurance to her gardening. But I was still on the books as a sub-under-deputy gardener.

'We need some trees.' The boundary to the left was a newish three-foot fence, which Mum thought a waste of a boundary. Even at eighty-two, as she was by now, she had a vision for the future. None of the "I'll not be here long" attitude with her.

We visited Everton Nurseries together, me by now having hired on a long-term basis a wheelchair to allow her to extend her trips out when I was involved. She chose four trees, none of which would grow more than a couple of feet in a year and I axed some holes in the concreted clay and flint (finding out for myself why nothing had been planted on that fence line) and planted the buggers. They'd barely moved on by the time she died, but she watered them religiously and stroked the new leaves that did appear with a tenderness she normally reserved for her grandchildren. Despite the conditions, at least they survived.

I can see her now, hefting a half full watering can to the first of those trees, before carefully emptying the contents around the base. She struggled to carry a full can and, of course, I offered. We both knew she didn't want my help. She knew how she wanted to water her trees and she didn't need my uncultured enthusiasm upsetting whatever delicate balance she had in mind. It might take her three, four times as long as it would me and I would probably get it more right than wrong, but why take the chance?

Mum didn't waste her energies. She didn't look for it, but she never eschewed hard work, far from it. She never gave into pain, never let it dictate to her or define her. But she saved her energies for where they were best needed. She understood both the art of delegation and the masculine need to provide and protect. Cunning as she was she would meld the two, tuning these two imposters to her – and let me be the first to admit, to my, one humble male's - advantage.

One afternoon, shortly before the tree project, the neighbour of the land at the end of the garden caught me. 'Hello, are you the son?'

'I suppose so.'

'Good. I spoke to your mother. I'm not sure she understood me.'

I knew that, wherever this conversation was going to go, it wasn't likely to end well for the neighbour. He continued. 'I want to buy your garden. From here.' He indicated a line about halfway down. 'I'll pay a fair price; I'm going to develop my plot and if I can get your garden I can get two, maybe three bungalows on it.'

It is perhaps difficult to paint a picture of how this might have worked, but it had, to me, many upsides.

Money, to start with.

A reduction in what was, frankly, a too big garden which even Mum recognised. A new fence and hedge at this man's cost. On the downside, Mum would lose the line of mature shrubs two thirds down. And she would be dealing, albeit through me, with this man.

'I'll talk to my mother.'

'Please. If you can explain how much mutual benefit there will be...' He sounded a little desperate.

Mum watched me, during this conversation. I joined her for tea. 'So, what did he offer?'

'He started at ten thousand.'

'Fool.'

'Him or me?'

She twinkled. 'You if you thought I'd sell.'

'You'd lose the shrubs.'

'True.' This said in a tone that evoked the wobbly hand gesture beloved of those suggesting you are close but not quite there.

'You'll be more overlooked.'

'Possibly.'

I hadn't nailed it yet. 'He said you probably didn't understand and could I explain.'

She nodded. That was the clincher. Mum would put up with a lot, but a patronising man was not one of them.

'I'll explain.'

'Make sure he understands. It may take you some time. I think I'll make some bread rolls; the marmalade seems to have settled well and just needs a fresh crust to set it off.'

In 1998, we took the children to Australia. We camped in Kakadu National Park where the Textiliste celebrated her fortieth birthday. This is Dad's tribute, with notes of Kipling and Roger McGough.

Birthday 'Down Under', 5th August 1998

Though neither a Homer not a Euripides,
Rudyard Kipling or Roger McGough,
I felt, since your birthday falls in the Antipodes,
Just a greeting card wasn't enough.
*

Barbara smiled – 'You're no budding Omar Khayyam,'
'Or Milton or Shakespeare,' she said,
'But you don't have to write Orwell's Animal Farm,'
Or verse with tremendous street cred.'
*

'You needn't produce some inspired interlude'
'In perfect iambic pentameter',
'Just your usual old stuff' – I thought that rather rude,
After all I'm only an amateur!
*

She's quite right of course – mine's a rough, homespun skill,
And Percy Bysshe Shelley I ain't,
And try as I might my verse remains still
Not so much clever as quaint.
*

So I will refrain from poetic thunder
'Cos Barbara and I want to say
Lots of love and good wishes to you there 'down under'
Many Happy Returns and – g'day!

Thirty-Six

Breaking The Code

Every family has its own secret code, nicknames, that sort of thing. I called Mum "Brian" for many years, based loosely on the snail in the 1960s children's stop motion filler called The Magic Roundabout. We also had words that were only understood within the circle of trust. One such came from the family's deep involvement with insects.

One thing I'm not sure Mum missed much, after Dad died, were his bugs. He loved all Lepidoptera and collected them throughout much of his life. I inherited his moth trap which died a death soon after I got it – I've recently replaced it, much to my family's joy. It's like he is still there, whenever we use it and open it in the morning to see what might have flown in overnight.

Back in the 1960s, when we first used a moth trap, we were inundated with small, rather drab moths. One task, for we enthusiasts, was identification and leading this charge was the Archaeologist. As with most tasks both then and now he read and read and absorbed what the experts over decades had to say.

After one collecting night yet another small unprepossessing moth remained unidentified. It was left to the Archaeologist to try and sort out what it was while Dad was at work. On returning home, Dad asked if he had had any joy.

'It's umbiquos,' reported a confident Archaeologist.

Dad, understandably, looked confused. 'Umbiquos?'

Not for the first time the Archaeologist had to explain to the less knowledgeable. 'It means very common.'

It took Dad a moment. 'Do you mean ubiquitous?'

As with a lot of family malapropisms these quickly become family lore, utilised like a secret language to confuse outsiders. I'm sure all families have them.

My father's mother, Nana, fulfilled her quota. The new sunglasses that became popular in the 1970s for their anti-glare were noted with "oh I would like some of those paranoid sunglasses" and when explaining where she lived to a taxi driver he was startled when she suggested he stop "just after the bollocks in the middle of the road".

The last I recall from when both my parents were still alive came courtesy of a piece of high disdain from Mum. As always, she'd been bullied by Dad to get ready for some rather formal trip out and had sneaked off to do some dead heading in the garden while he fussed over the directions or the invite or what wine to take.

Finally, he realised where she was and in exasperation called her in. 'Barbs, for heaven's sake. Aren't you ready yet?'

'Of course,' protested Mum.

'Well, what's that on your shoulders? Looks like dandruff.'

Mum didn't even bother to look. As she strode past him, brushing each shoulder swiftly, she explained, 'It's pollen.'

Dad, for once, was floored, though later he had his revenge by calling her "pollen" as a term of endearment thereafter. Mum would smile sweetly, but they both understood the joke, one they kept to themselves.

And why did I call her Brian? Well, if you saw the hat he wore and saw Mum's... Anyway, it suited her and she rather enjoyed it.

Thirty-Seven

Memoriam

I often wondered how Dad would have dealt with Mum's funeral. He would have been expected to craft a poem; everyone he knew called upon him to provide part of the 'entertainment' for events happy and sad. He would have been torn into shreds, but still have been desperate not to let people down. This was brought into stark relief with the tragic death of his best friend Les Kench.

Dad maintained many friendships throughout his life, but the one that formed after we first moved to Hampshire was probably the deepest and most enduring. Les was an engineer who worked at the same chemical plant as Dad. He was a marvel with cars, loved beer and had a great sense of humour. His and Dad's rivalry over who grew the best vegetables continued across decades.

Tragically Les died next to Dad as he and Mum drove Les and his wife, Sylvia to Heathrow. It shattered them all. It was, we all knew, inevitable that Sylvia would ask Dad to say something at Les' memorial service in Lymington.

Dad didn't want to; he was really reluctant which everyone, but Mum found a surprise – astonishing almost. But the reason was typical of the man; he feared – no, he knew - he would cry. It was utterly inevitable. And to do so would let down both himself and his friendship with Les, a friendship that was founded on the most deeply felt convictions of manliness that they both espoused.

When I realised what was bothering him (Mum dropped an atom-bomb-sized hint), I called him immediately and told him – in my best lawyerly tones – not to be so bloody selfish. Of course he'd cry. Everyone was going to be in floods for Les was the epitome of a gentle man. But, and here's the thing, crying, breaking down for someone who was so important to Dad, and knowing how hard he, Les, would have teased Dad about it if he could have, was the ultimate compliment to as good a friend as a man could have.

Dad agreed and then couldn't decide on what to say. Once again, we had words; I said it had to be rude, it had to tease, at least somewhere in it because everyone understood that was their relationship and to ignore that would not fairly reflect the man. 'Only you can do that, Dad,' I said.

This, and I'm suppressing a tear as I write this, is what he said. And yes, he wept. He had to stop twice to recover his composure. And everyone who could, came and thanked him for this, especially Sylvia. When it's my turn to be the centre of attention like this, I rather hope that one of the many friends I've abused down the years will find their way to even half as good a tribute.

Memorial To A Friend

Les, today we grieve, for you are not among us,
But I for one will not stay sad for long,
For my memories down the years are of happy times, not tears,
And to pipe my eye too much would be so wrong.
*

We were different, and alike, in very many ways,
But I can recognise the better man,
And if quality's a race then you're right there in first place
Way ahead of most of us – the 'also rans'.
*

We shared a love of England and the older, country ways,
And our experiences in youth were much the same,
We took several trips abroad and I'm sure our wives got bored
With our chaffing which was all part of the game.
*

I like walking, you liked golf but our waistlines both have spread,
We enjoyed good food, a pint, a glass of wine,
And in the pub on Monday nights we'd put the world to rights,
And still be arguing come closing time.
*

In our gardens we were rivals, no quarter asked or given,
(And I still say I grow better runner beans)
But when the problem was mechanic you could cope while I would
panic
And I still don't know what carburettor means.
*

I recall our shared delight in that final, super Test
At the Oval, watching England pile on the score,
And at Twickenham, of course, we cheered till we were hoarse
At the try that clinched the Triple Crown once more.
*

176

So how can I be sad with such good times to remember,
Certainly that wouldn't be your choice.
And, if memory stays kind, I can always call to mind
Your happy, laughing face and cheery voice.
*

But, just for today, old friend, we grieve a little for you are not among
us.

Thirty-Eight

The Final Curtain

Mum's birthday was, she was proud to tell anyone, Trafalgar Day - 21st October. She exulted in British History and, while not completely dewy-eyed as to the wondrous gift to the world that was the British Empire (her view), she considered, on balance, it was a good thing. For her, things such as the rule of law, parliamentary democracy, the stability that comes with a constitutional monarchy, outweighed the concomitant exploitation, the suppression of local language and culture and the imposition that arbitrary and ill-thought out borders might have on a people. She was of a generation, like our current monarch, that considers duty to be the standard and to have "done one's duty" to be the highest accolade. Sitting in regal splendour at the end of a large table at the restaurant that was formerly Holmsley railway station, surrounded by her family - the Archaeologist and me and our spouses, her brother, his children and her grandchildren - she shone. She wanted for no present, no praise beyond just to be there, a curly-haired smiley penumbra to their many sparkles and hopes. She was eighty-four and as content as her many niggles allowed.

In my memory it was sunny after rain, that October lunchtime. I'm sure she had fish and chips with extra tartar sauce, a glass of white and a coffee to follow. It was her usual fayre. She smiled and nodded and occasionally lost her focus, perhaps wondering at what her darling husband would have said, what teasing he would undertake on such an occasion.

Did we take her home or was it the Archaeologist? Surely, we all went back to hers where scones or a cake or both awaited. With tea. Of course, with tea. We chatted, maybe we snoozed and finally left her to it in the early evening to drive back to London.

Little did I know that was probably the last time I saw her on such "good form", an expression she would use often. Sometime after this came the shenanigans with her car when I discovered the truth about her clutch-punishment and we began to explore the options for an automatic. Looking back, the fact she was so compliant about our suggestion that she needed to change should have been a clue. Mum didn't really do "compliant". Silent rebellion for sure but never compliance.

It would be in mid-November that my aunt's number came up on my phone. She is one forthright lady, my aunt, calling a spade an effing shovel as her default. I expected chastisement for some unheralded misdemeanour - she usually rang when I was in the wrong - but I didn't expect her to say, before even the slimmest of greetings, 'You need to get down here. Barbara needs you.'

I was in Suffolk, on a beach. "Here" was the south coast on the other side of Southampton. It was a Sunday afternoon. My job had changed by then and I was part of the legal team trying to bring sanity to the madness that was the 2012 London Olympics. At that particular moment, I was up to my gills in issues around the wrap on the Olympic Stadium and the stupid Kapoor sculpture, the Orbit, which still looks like some heavenly jazz combo has dropped its trombone into the Olympic Park - I had papers to read that evening for some meetings early on Monday. 'Why?' I asked, rather defensively.

What she told me shook me. She hadn't heard from Mum for a few days - to my everlasting shame I hadn't spoken to her in over a week, given the pressure I'd been under at LOCOG.

Aunt found Mum in her chair in the sitting room. Sort of spaced, not really engaged. It was clear she'd not eaten or, well, moved in a while. She was very confused. Subsequently it turned out she had a major bladder infection and a blockage that needed an operation. That's a classic combination that leads to confusion in the elderly.

All of us were relying on the fact that there were others who contacted her and because she'd always been so strong, so together, we assumed she'd tell us if she needed us. Those few days of uncalled for neglect are days I wish I could take back.

The Archaeologist dropped everything and went over that evening. I went down the next day. Her GP - a wonderfully supportive man - came straight out and had her into Bournemouth Hospital in a trice. Her care was splendid and, initially, her treatment stabilised her.

For all her personal traits Mum hadn't been well for decades, never free of some complication. After being diagnosed with rheumatoid arthritis, she was told the prognosis was that she would, likely, end up in a wheelchair. At that time, however, there were some new albeit fairly experimental treatments which, while they worked for her, came with appalling side effects, one being significantly raised blood pressure. The result was she medicated, pretty constantly. Never was she short of a pill or two.

By the time of her bladder issue the medication had changed and the blood pressure was stable - happy days, she could drink champagne again, famously saving her extra winter fuel allowance, awarded by Gordon Brown, to buy herself a half bottle of Moët with which she toasted the Chancellor on Christmas Day - but her heart was weakened and a kidney had given up the ghost.

As the year wound down to a gloomy mouldy December there were tests and operations discussed. She nodded and let the Archaeologist and me make decisions. She stayed with us at Christmas that year and barely moved from her bed, now placed downstairs. But she held court with her grandchildren and they engaged her as only young people can.

I took her home, and the Archaeologist, my aunt and uncle and their family took over the care with a nurse who came in. We waited for news of her bladder operation, her stent, as the year flipped over into 2010.

And then the news I was dreading. A call from a breathless brother. Mum was in hospital, Bournemouth again, having an emergency operation. She had a duodenal ulcer that had burst. Who knew? Another problem, another major pain which she'd never mentioned, never complained about.

I left it a day - my brother was there and she was in recovery in an ICU - before I visited. She was being held in an induced coma and the specialists, while pleased with the operation, were worried about her general ability to recover.

A day or two later - time slips and segues on these occasions, sometimes marching double time, sometimes dragging funereally - an anxious young man in stripy shirt and stethoscope asked for a word. Mum's second kidney had failed. To start it, they needed her heart to pump extra blood, but if they tried to stimulate it it too began to fail. She was too old for a transplant even if she could have coped with the operation, and long-term dialysis was not really an option.

As he took me through all the options, I looked at Mum, apparently sleeping peacefully surrounded by a bank of machines. Mum was an active woman. Even when trapped by her arthritis she cooked, sewed and filled her days with smiles and friends. If she couldn't recover to something approximating her current situation, how happy would she be?

The doctor's face posed the question without asking it. Do we continue keeping her going, powered by modern technology, in some forlorn hope of a recovery from who knew where or do we let her go?

Of course, the answer was obvious, but even so, how fair is it to be the person to choose? Then again, I've had to decide to have beloved pets put down and isn't this the human equivalent? For whose benefit do I insist on continuing the status quo? Isn't that cowardice?

I called the Archaeologist. My relationship with my brother has grown stronger and deeper over the years, but these are the moments they are tested. Can I say he was marvellous then? He's not the most empathetic of people, or so it can seem, but that belies a sensitive core. It's more he has trouble articulating feelings, rather than not having them. But not then. He was logical and kind, as aware of how difficult I was finding this as he must have been. After all we were deciding to become orphans. It was on us.

It took two days; she slipped away in the wee hours of a Thursday morning. The hospital rang - I stayed at her bungalow while this happened - the call came in shortly before six. I wasn't exactly getting a good night's rest.

I called close family, then sat and drank tea and watched the sun slowly rise over her neglected garden. It was going to be a dry clear day. At just before nine my phone rang. An engineer called Rory, at the Olympics, anxious to discuss a lift engineering contract with me. I listened to his irrelevant worries and gave him some advice. I don't think it was particularly sensible, all things considered, but oddly it helped break me from the fug of maudlin thoughts that had enveloped me.

Time to get on with the day, with life. It's what she would have wanted, indeed demanded; after all, in her eyes, it was never about her.

Afterword: At some point while she was in the ICU she emerged from her coma, briefly, to smile at me. Her smile, sans teeth, would have horrified her - she had some personal vanity - and it was accompanied by what turned out to be her last words:

Hello, darling.

Appropriate we should end on a greeting, wrapped up in love.

October 21st, 1995

You are:
Lover, friend, companion, mother to my boys, listener to my troubles,
shoulder to cry on, foil for my bad temper, book keeper, gardener,

upstairs/downstairs and in between, maid, housekeeper, doctor and nurse, hostess when required, accountant, banker, carpenter, painter and decorator, tailor and seamstress, chauffeuse, caterpillar-feeder, economist, bricklayer, laugher at my jokes, restorer of my confidence – and so much more.

Thank you, my darling.

About the author

Geoff Le Pard is a former lawyer, a novelist, an enthusiastic blogger (at https://geofflepard.com/), someone who enjoys walking and talking at length and a lover of London. He walks miles with his dog while they both seek their own inspiration. He published his first book, Dead Flies and Sherry Trifle, in late 2014, his second, My Father and Other Liars, in August 2015, his third, Salisbury Square, in late 2016 and his latest, Buster & Moo, in July 2017. His first anthology he wrote as a challenge: 30 stories in 30 days. Life, in a Grain of Sand, was published in June 2016. His second, Life In A Flash, was published in 2017. All his books are available on Amazon as both eBooks and paperbacks.

Acknowledgements

Many people helped me on my writing journey, but for this memoir I must thank my family for their patience and fortitude in allowing me to dig into our collective history in order to create these images of my parents. Memory is a fragile and often fickle thing and when, as inevitably they will, they find something that they remember differently then I ask their understanding and forgiveness.

I must say a heartfelt thank you to Esther Clinton (Editing Services) for her expertise in editing this work and George Grey (Royalston Design) for the stunning cover.

The proceeds of the sale of all my books will be donated to charity.

34222502R00109

Printed in Great Britain
by Amazon